Multiculturalism and Education

2nd Edition

The Companion Website relating to this book is available online at: http://
www.bloomsbury.com/uk/multiculturalism-and-education-9781472570185/

If you experience any problems accessing the Companion Website, please
contact Bloomsbury at companionwebsites@bloomsbury.com

Contemporary Issues in Education Studies

Series editors: Richard Race and Simon Pratt-Adams

This series presents an authoritative, coherent and focused collection of core texts to introduce the contemporary issues that are covered in Education Studies, and related programmes.

Each book develops a key theme in contemporary education, such as:

– Multiculturalism
– The social construction of childhood
– Urban education
– eLearning and multimedia
– Language and literacy

A key feature of this series is the critical exploration of education in times of rapid change, with links made between such developments in wider social, cultural, political and economic contexts. Further, contextualized extracts from important primary texts, such as Bourdieu, Piaget and Vygotsky, will ensure students' exposure to dominant contemporary theories in the field of education.

Grounded in a strong conceptual, theoretical framework and presented in an accessible way with the use of features such as case studies, activities and visual devices to encourage and support student learning and the application of new concepts, this series will serve well as collection of core texts for the Education Studies student and lecturer.

Titles in the series:

Also available from Bloomsbury

Multiculturalism and Education

2nd Edition

Richard Race

Contemporary Issues in Education Studies

Bloomsbury Academic
An imprint of Bloomsbury Publishing Plc

BLOOMSBURY
LONDON · NEW DELHI · NEW YORK · SYDNEY

Bloomsbury Academic
An imprint of Bloomsbury Publishing Plc

50 Bedford Square	1385 Broadway
London	New York
WC1B 3DP	NY 10018
UK	USA

www.bloomsbury.com

BLOOMSBURY and the Diana logo are trademarks of Bloomsbury Publishing Plc

First edition published 2010 by the Continuum International Publishing Group Ltd

This edition published 2015

British Library Cataloguing-in-Publication Data
A catalogue record for this book is available from the British Library.

ISBN: HB: 978-1-4725-7019-2
      PB: 978-1-4725-7018-5
    ePub: 978-1-4725-7021-5
    ePDF: 978-1-4725-7020-8

Library of Congress Cataloging-in-Publication Data
Race, Richard.
 Multiculturalism and education / Richard Race. – Second edition.
   pages cm. – (Contemporary issues in education studies)
 Includes bibliographical references and index.
 ISBN 978-1-4411-1326-9 (hardback) – ISBN 978-1-84706-018-1 (pbk.)
 1. Education–Social aspects–Great Britain. 2. Multiculturalism–Great Britain.
 3. Multicultural education–Great Britain. I. Title.
  LC191.8.G7R34 2014
  370.117–dc23
                                            2014026841

Series: Contemporary Issues in Education Studies

Typeset by Newgen Knowledge Works (P) Ltd., Chennai, India
Printed and bound in India

Contents

vi   Contents

Series Editors' Preface to the First Edtion

The series *Contemporary Issues in Education Studies* is timely for its critical exploration of education in this period of accelerating change. Responding to this challenge, the books in the series have titles which correspond closely to the needs of students taking a wide range of courses and modules within Education Studies and related fields such as teacher education. Education Studies is an important subject area and should be at the heart of many faculties of education. There is a need for relevant, core texts within Education Studies, which explore and critique contemporary issues across the discipline and challenge prevailing discourses of what education is about. We also need to provide students with strong theoretical perspectives and frameworks, focusing on relevant literature in an accessible and readable format.

We set the authors of this series a number of challenges in terms of what to include in their text. Therefore, each book addresses a contemporary issue in education and has an international rather than just an English focus. The texts are structured to provide a clear grasp of the topic and to provide an overview of research, current debates and perspectives. Contextualized extracts from important primary texts ensure readers' exposure to dominant contemporary theories in the field of education, by demystifying essential vocabulary and educational discourse, enabling the education student to engage with these texts in a meaningful way. The extensive and appropriate literature review in each text gives a firm base for contextualizing the subject and promoting understanding at multiple levels.

This series is grounded in a strong conceptual, theoretical framework and is presented in an accessible way. Each book uses features such as case studies, reflective exercises and activities that encourage and support student learning. Key relevant and contemporary questions are inserted throughout each chapter to extend the readers' thinking and understanding. Furthermore, additional material is also provided in the companion website to each book.

The text *Multiculturalism and Education* is solely authored by Richard Race who writes from extensive multi-disciplinary experience, gained from working in universities in England, The Netherlands, The Republic of Ireland and Greece. A diverse range of students have been found in these educational environments. The author's practitioner knowledge as Programme Convenor for the MA in Education at Roehampton University and research experiences on: education history; the relationship between education politicians and civil servants; and, the concept of teacher professionalism enabled data to be collected from a sample of people working and interested in multicultural education. The empirical data was collected through the distribution of 3 different questionnaires and 33 semi-structured interviews. The informants provided insights concerning the contemporary relevance of the issues being addressed in this book, that is: faith schooling; the development of citizenship; and, the debates surrounding the argument for promoting multiculturalism within educational contexts.

The book analyses the continuing influence of educational debates surrounding inclusion and diversity. The ongoing conceptual analysis of different ideas, which include assimilation, integration, anti-racism, helps to explain the evolution and development of multiculturalism. These ideas are then applied to different English education and social policy documents including Every Child Matters. Trevor Phillips' 2005 speech on multiculturalism and segregation is also examined in the book. Issues described by Phillips, that is, integration are important when reflecting on multiculturalism because they challenge the focal concept being examined. The difference concerning an integrationist conditional relationship between the state and individual, which involves terms such as responsibility, duty; and tolerance in education policy documents will be highlighted alongside a multicultural celebration of cultural diversity. Phillip's also touches on reducing social and cultural segregation but misses other issues covered in this book, for example, community cohesion.

For several years, the author of this book has been promoting the possibilities of citizenship education in conference presentations and other publications. This book suggests citizenship debates can be developed in classrooms and seminar rooms which offer the greatest potential for developing multicultural ideas.

Multiculturalism and Education underlines the need to understand and continue to advance the idea of multiculturalism within societies. This book is crucial not only for students, but for all professional practitioners. As in other books in the series, we challenge and encourage the reader to think critically and differently about education. The challenge in this book focuses on the need to not only recognize changing cultural diversity, but to promote change within citizenship and other curriculum subjects which positively promotes and celebrates our multicultural world.

Simon Pratt-Adams and Richard Race
September 2010
London

Preface to the Second Edition

This second edition of Multiculturalism and Education is published at a significant time when immigration is again being used as a political devise to deflect attention away from issues concerning the changing cultural diversities in England and around the world. The response to the first edition of this book from colleagues and students within the United Kingdom and around the world, as well as Stephen McKinney and Paul Thomas who reviewed the book in the *Journal of Education Policy* and *Educational Review* has been extremely positive and measured which was another incentive to write the new material for the second edition. The movement from multicultural to integrationist citizenship as a conceptual and policy development, is analysed by looking at political theory, political speeches and citizenship education curriculum in England. The new material underlines the need to continue to look at multiculturalism and education as well as the growing important idea of integration and how it has shaped and continues to shape social and education policy-making. The need to look at other ideas and concepts such as assimilation, separation, anti-racism, anti-discrimination, human rights and apply them to curriculum subjects remains as it increases our understandings of how complex policy-making processes are but also how the state shapes policy politically to influence the decisions we all make.

The current political climate in England and across Europe suggests that this movement from multicultural to integrationist-inspired policy is in fact turning towards a more exclusive view of the nation state in a political sense rather than a more multicultural, inclusive examination of the global realities of the twenty-first century. The political speeches of Merkel, Cameron and Clegg highlight the differences in integrationist and multicultural focuses. Merkel skilfully recognized multiculturalism in Germany but promoted a more integrationist position, appealing successfully to the cultural diversity of the German electorate. It remains to be seen whether Cameron and Clegg and their different positions on integration, immigration and multiculturalism will be enough to convince the UK electorate to make them electable in the May 2015 General Election. It is interesting to compare Cameron and Clegg's speeches examined in Chapter 7 while remembering the political pride expressed in a multicultural, culturally diverse Britain that held the Olympics in London in 2012.

What also needs to be highlighted, in an English context, is what has changed concerning multiculturalism and education since the publication of the first edition of this book. It is important to underline what new powers the Education Act (DfE, 2011) has given Coalition politicians. The significant closure of the Qualification and Curriculum Development Agency (QCDA) and the creation of the Office of Qualifications and Examinations Regulation (OfQual) can be seen with OfQual in June 2014 opening a debate questioning the inclusion and consequent assessment of subjects that are deemed irrelevant within education. The Secretary of State for Education is now not only entitled to open debates on what can be taught in the National Curriculum, including history and modern foreign languages as well as what texts can be taught in English Literature; but s/he can change curriculum because s/he has the executive authority to do so. What needs to be highlighted here is not the possible replacement of books by Harper Lee, Arthur Miller or John Steinbeck in future English Literature curricula within the new GCSE English qualification. The fact is that Michael Gove and from July 2014 his successor, Nicky Morgan, has the power to do this as curriculum decisions were brought back into the Department for Education as a consequence of the Education Act (DfE, 2011) closing the QCDA down.

In the current political climate, not just in England but around the world, we have to be continuously careful how our ideas and thoughts concerning immigration processes are shaped politically because they influence and shape education policy-making. One of the major arenas where thoughts and ideas can be developed remains the classroom and lecture theatre. In relation to multicultural education, professional practitioners have to continue to promote curricula and professional practice that underlines the importance of culturally diverse practice, through diversity training that allows us to develop our own inclusive professional practice. We also have to increase our understandings of how integration has and continues to be used by the nation state to preserve monocultural values which seemingly become more redundant as information technology within globalization brings the world even closer together. Despite this and to the contrary, the nation state continues to create education policy that aims to keep the nation state together for example a national curriculum in England that has recently been revised and will be introduced into over 90 per cent of state-maintained schools in England in 2014–2015. This conditional two-way integrationist relationship between the state and policy-making on the one hand, with individuals and groups responding, or not responding on the other hand, is the integrationist reality that modern state policy continues to deliver. It is these processes that involve integration and education policy-making that I will continue to examine in current and future research. The new finding of this edition is that actual curriculum content in all subjects needs to be researched to increase understandings how subjects change, evolve or do not evolve over time. Despite my evolving focus on the conceptual ideas on integration and assimilation – not because I agree with them but because I believe they have more contemporary influence on education policy-making – I continue to advocate and develop a teaching and learning method based upon: method; depth; and, reach for all professional practitioners that has multiculturalism as its cornerstone within all education subjects.

Richard Race
Syros, Greece, August 2014

Acknowledgements

The School of Education at Roehampton University has always been a place of opportunities and possibilities. I would like to thank: Elise Alexander; Farkhanda Anjum; Ron Best; Lynne Bradley; Penny Jane Burke; Sandra Craig; Gill Crozier; Alaster Douglas; Becky Francis; Dianne Gereluk; Sue Greenfield; Julie Hall; Elaine Hilides; Marilyn Holness; Jeanne Keay; Nick Langford; Anastasia Liasidou; Pat Mahony; Ada Mau; Tristan McCowan; Jackie Moses; Carol Neill; Jackie Nunn; Hayley Noakes; Jo Peat; Lawrie Price; Barbara Read; Sue Robson; David Rose; Mary Richardson; Cathy Svensson; Julie Shaughnessy; Lorella Terzi; and, Anthony Thorpe.

To all members of the British Education Research Association (BERA) Special Interest Group (SIG) in Race and Ethnicity in Education and in particular: Khalwant Bhopal; Charlotte Chadderton; Nick Johnson; Shamim Miah; John Preston; and, Jasmine Rhamie. Many thanks to Vini Lander who I co-convened the SIG with between 2010–2013.

As co-director of Postgraduate Training Programmes at Roehampton University, I've been lucky to deliver the MA in both domestic and international education settings. I would like to thank: Jos Bergkamp; Evi Botsari; Martin Kessels; Christian Mortimore; Julia Shepard; Phil Skittides; and, Jacqueline van Swet.

For comments, guidance, support and inspiration concerning this book, I would like to thank: Floya Anthias; Jackie Brown; Barbara Cole; John Eade; Gill Forrester; Dave Gillborn; Helen Gunter; Ken Jones; Stephen McKinney; Jane Parish; Chris Phillipson; Michael Singh; and, Handel Wright. I'd also like to thank Steven Emm for proof reading the final draft.

I'd like to thank my co-editor, Simon Pratt-Adams for his friendship and professional support in the development of this book (first and second edition) and series. Special thanks to all the other authors in the Series, as well as Alison Baker, Frances Arnold and Rachel Eisenhauer at Bloomsbury.

This book is dedicated not only to family and friends, but all the students who I have lectured at Keele; Liverpool John Moores; London Metropolitan; St Mary's College, Strawberry Hill and Roehampton. The last words go to Alexandra Xanthaki who helped me clarify legal issues in the new material, still the bravest person I know and has given me a unique insight into our multicultural world. *My eyes, my Alexandra.*

Introduction

Introduction

The contemporary issue of multiculturalism and its importance within current education debates is dealt with here. The aim of this book is to increase understandings of how multiculturalism has conceptually developed over time and how applications of the term have shaped education debates (Banks, 2009). The book is also part of an ongoing debate on multiculturalism within education and the social sciences which includes other concepts that is, integration and citizenship. As Race (in Eade et al., 2008: 1) wrote, 'Multiculturalism *still* matters and is even more important after 7/7 [and 9/11] than it was before'. This quote suggests that conceptual debates can not only allow us to test our ideas and theories about society, but also allow us to focus on contemporary issues that surround us in all subject areas, including education. In this book, that will involve not only an examination of multiculturalism and its continued evolution as a concept, but also the consequences multiculturalism has had on different education issues, for example faith schools and citizenship within not only the national curriculum in England but also in other countries around the world.

In relation to multiculturalism and education, the notion of cultural diversity is important and significant as are notions of identity and difference. For Parekh (2000: 2–3), culture is, '. . . a body of beliefs and practices in terms of which a group of people understand themselves and the world they organize their individual and collective lives around'. Identity and difference are interlinked with multiculturalism as Parekh (2000: 3) highlights when he states that multiculturalism is about cultural diversity or culturally embedded differences. As Bolton (2010: 67) underlines: 'We are all culture bound – physically, socially, psychologically and spiritually. We might change that culture, but can never make ourselves culture free'. So, there is no escape from culture, as there is no escape from multiculture, which is described by Pathak (2008) as the celebration of difference in contemporary life.

When attempting to examine cultural diversity, multiculturalism and education, empirical data has been collected for this book to test ideas from the existing literature. Questionnaires and interviews were created and data was collected from a domestic and international group from the fields of education and social science under the following categories: university lecturers; university teacher trainers and teacher trainees; undergraduate and postgraduate students and, members of interest groups involved with the promotion of multicultural education. Data was collected from 20 questionnaires and 33 interviews and the comments expressed by these respondents assisted in increasing understandings of multiculturalism and education. The viewpoints drawn from the respondent data and the reflective exercises found in the chapters of this book have been created to challenge the reader to become 'critically reflective' (Harrison in Dymoke and Harrison, 2008: 37; Fook and Gardner, 2007) and create conditions in current or future practice to make multiculturalism more visible, practical and inclusive for both students and teachers within education at all levels.

Defining multiculturalism and a multicultural perspective

This section highlights the main debates which help us to define multiculturalism and develop a multicultural perspective. Multiculturalism as a concept has different histories and origins in different countries. Canada was the first country in the world to adopt multiculturalism as an official policy in 1971, in an attempt, as Day (2002: 18–23) suggests, to achieve unity through diversity. It is interesting to look at how the contemporary Canadian government defines the concept:

> Canadian multiculturalism is fundamental to our belief that all citizens are equal. Multiculturalism ensures that all citizens can keep their identities, can take pride in their ancestry and have a sense of belonging. Acceptance gives Canadians a feeling of security and self-confidence, making them more open to, and accepting of, diverse cultures. The Canadian experience has shown that multiculturalism encourages racial and ethnic harmony and cross-cultural understanding, and discourages ghettoization, hatred, discrimination and violence. (CIC, 2009)

It is an impressive definition and theoretically has a wide-ranging cultural and social significance. Recognition and acceptance of differences in law and the discouragement of discrimination and racism is fundamental in any country that believes all citizens are equal. Conceptual debates within the Canadian state concerning multiculturalism have promoted the issues of equal and human rights alongside debates which address issues of ghettoization and violence (CDSoS, 1987; CMoSMC, 1991). On the one hand, Day (2002: 1) argues that, '. . . while Canadian multiculturalism presents itself as a new solution to an ancient problem of diversity, it is better seen as the most recent mode of *reproduction* and *proliferation* of that problem' (For more details on aspects of Canadian multiculturalism see Johnson and Enomoto, 2007; Biles et al., 2008). Canada comes close as Adam-Moodley (1986: 13) suggests when comparing the education systems of Germany, South Africa and Canada, to '. . . satisfying the educational aspirations of both the majority and minority in an ethically divided society . . .'. From the comparative education example above, it seems that Canada, as a state, has come close to not only defining but trying to implement multicultural policies based on equal rights. As Day (2002) points out, these processes have not been perfect and the debates continue as Canada, like other countries, continues to culturally change and become more diverse. Multiculturalism in the United States is defined by Banks and Banks as:

> A philosophical position and movement that assumes that the gender, ethnic, racial, and cultural diversity of a pluralistic society should be reflected in all of the institutionalised structures of educational institutions, including the

> staff, the norms and values, the curriculum and the students body. (Banks and Banks, 2007: 474)

Multiculturalism, in England, is seen by Parekh as a perspective on human life and contains central insights into how we socially construct our lives:

- First, human beings are culturally embedded in the sense that they grow up and live within a culturally structured world, organize their lives and social relations in terms of its system of meaning and significance, and place considerable value on their cultural identity . . .
- Second, different cultures represent different systems of meaning and visions of the good life. Since each realizes a limited range of human capacities and emotions and grasps only a part of the totality of human existence, it needs others to understand itself better [and] expand its intellectual and moral horizon . . .
- Third, all but the most primitive cultures are . . . plural and represent a continuing conversation between their different traditions and strands of thought. This does not mean that they are devoid of internal coherence and identity but that their identity is plural and fluid. (Parekh, 2000: 336–37)

What Parekh calls a multicultural perspective is,

> composed of the creative interplay of these three complementary insights, namely the cultural embeddedness of human beings, the inescapability and desirability of cultural diversity and intercultural dialogue, and the internal plurality of each culture . . . From a multicultural perspective, no political doctrine or ideology can represent the full truth of human life. (Parekh, 2000: 338)

Acknowledging the above definitions from Banks and Banks (2007) as well as Parekh (2000) of multiculturalism which highlight different social constructions and educational structures, the aim of taking forward the notion of cultural diversity within a pluralistic society is useful. This multicultural perspective underlines the recognition of gender, ethnicity and race,[1] alongside the desirability of cultural diversity and the internal plurality of cultures. Baber (2008: 9) offers an interesting critique of multiculturalism claiming that, '. . . most people do not want to live in a plural monoculturalist "salad bowl" '. That salad bowl metaphor – an image to highlight different ethnic groups in modern America which symbolized the ingredients which contributed to the salad – was created to produce a multicultural image but had a monocultural impact which did not aim to focus on different cultures. Multiculturalism, at the very least, is a desirable acknowledgement of cultural diversity within a pluralistic society.

One of the major issues that this book seeks to address is whether the concept of multiculturalism does or can go further than this. Baber (2008: 14–19) suggests that the alternative in the United States to multiculturalism is integration and assimilation within schools and neighbourhoods. It would be disagreeable to support Baber's suggestion that by returning to the past and revising assimilation or integration educational and social policies, we can begin to address issues concerning cultural diversity. The conceptual debate concerning assimilation, integration and multiculturalism is examined in the next chapter of this book.

At this stage, let us reassert the Canadian state position (CIC, 2009) of a multiculturalism that promotes equal rights and discourages discrimination, agree with Banks and Banks (2007) that multiculturalism cannot be thought of as a single concept which is socially on its own, and also agree with Parekh (2000) and his claim that multiculturalism is both plural and fluid which recognizes how cultural diversity is constantly changing. Educational structures and agents – meaning for example, the state, schools, colleges, universities, teachers, children and parents – all need to acknowledge how culture continues to change. However, changing educational structures like an education system to incorporate greater cultural diversity through a curriculum (DES, 1985; DfES, 2007) and changing the agents' perspectives to acknowledge that multiculturalism can be difficult when considering economic issues alongside the fluid nature of cultural diversity when considering an issue that is, the promotion of equal educational rights (Banks, 2009).

Multicultural education

Having introduced the key general debates concerning multiculturalism we now move to the more specific debates concerning multicultural education. Banks (2004; 2007; 2009) and Parekh (2000; 2008) have played a crucial part in the development and promotion of multicultural education all over the world. For Banks (in Modgil et al., 1986: 222), multicultural education '. . . is an inclusive concept used to describe a wide variety of school practices, programs and materials designed to help children from diverse groups to experience educational equality . . . '. It's interesting to reflect on the date of the above quote as it is nearly 25 years old at the time of writing this book, which shows to the reader how long these ongoing issues have been debated. Banks (ibid.) mentions how multicultural education deals, or attempts to deal with 'serious problems in society' but can 'evoke strong emotions, feelings and highly polarize opinions'. In many respects, that previous comment is one of the many justifications for this book. Data collected for this book from completed questionnaires and interviews focused upon issues concerning multiculturalism and multicultural education. Parekh (in Taylor, 1988b: 14–16) suggests that multicultural education is, '. . . a way of avoiding . . . mistakes . . . and cultivating such capacities as mutual respect, intellectual curiosity, dialogue, self-criticism and quest for critical self-knowledge'. Education systems contain many sites for example, primary or secondary schools, where these personal capacities can be developed or blocked. As Parekh (ibid.) shows, '. . . the school is part of society which is . . . characterised by specific ways of thought and life that is a specific historically evolved culture . . . '. Then to this extent, education is indeed monocultural. It is the multicultural reality within education that Parekh is interested in. He continues to point out that:

- First, no culture, at least not in such a developed and self-critical society as Britain, is a monolithic and undifferentiated unit . . .
- Second, common culture is not a static entity. It is constantly exposed to new needs and influences, and evolves, acquires new sensibilities and makes appropriate internal adjustments in response to them . . .
- The third dimension of multicultural education relates to what we teach, and how. There is no good reason why our syllabus should not be made more broad-based than at present . . . . (ibid.)

Parekh suggests within the plural, fluid nature of British cultural diversity and society, the important education issue concerning multiculturalism is what we teach in the curriculum and how we teach it. Parekh wrote these ideas down after the publication of the Swann Report (DES, 1985) having been a member of the committee set up to report on 'Education for All'. This education policy document will be examined in more depth in the next chapter but it is significant that these three points above still apply to education today. The implication from Parekh's evidence is that the recommendations from the Swann Report (DES, 1985) do not apply or incorporate multicultural ideas within education.

The most comprehensive analysis of multicultural education and the differing conceptual positions that concern research on the pedagogy of multicultural education are underlined under five headings with selected explanations in bullet points by Steinberg and Kincheloe shown in the box below:

1. Conservative multiculturalism or monoculturalism
   - *tends to believe in the superiority of Western patriarchal culture;*
   - *sees the children of the poor and non-white as culturally deprived;*
   - *attempts to assimilate everyone capable of assimilation to a Western, middle/upper-class-standard.*

2. Liberal multiculturalism
   - *emphasizes the natural equality and common humanity of individuals from diverse race, class, and gender groups;*
   - *argues that inequality results from a lack of opportunity;*
   - *claims ideological neutrality on the basis that politics should be separated from education;*
   - *accepts the assimilationist goals of conservative multiculturalism.*

3. Pluralist multiculturalism
   - *. . . focuses more on race, class, and gender differences rather than similarities;*
   - *contends that the curriculum should consist of studies of various divergent groups;*
   - *promotes pride in group heritage.*

4. Left-essential multiculturalism
   - *defines groups and membership in groups around the barometer of authenticity (fidelity to the unchanging priorities of the historical group in question);*
   - *romanticizes the group, in the process erasing the complexity and diversity of its history;*
   - *often is involved in struggles with other subjected groups over whose oppression is most elemental [and] takes precedence over all other forms.*

5. Critical multiculturalism
   - *grounds a critical pedagogy that promotes an understanding of how schools / education work by the exposure of student sorting processes and power's complicity with the curriculum;*
   - *rejects the assumption that education provides consistent socio-economic mobility for working-class and non-white students;*
   - *identifies what gives rise to race, class, and gender inequalities.*

(Steinberg and Kincheloe in Steinberg (ed.), 2001: 3–5)

Headings four and five in Steinberg and Kincheloe (2001) suggest the possibilities of multiculturalism and its usage in education. The bullet points give the reader a general idea of how different views and standpoints on multicultural education can be applied to different education systems. The English system of education, as we shall examine in the next chapter, has historically evolved and taken elements of the first four points from the above headings. Parekh (2000) has already made a case for pluralist multiculturalism. Kincheloe and Steinberg (1997: 28) favour a critical multiculturalism which moves beyond focusing on culturally diverse practice and moves towards how, '. . . racism, sexism and class bias are economically, semiotically (pertaining to encoded and symbolic representations of particular groups), politically, educationally and institutionally produced'. We all need to be interested in the above headings from Steinberg and Kincheloe (2001) because they help to explain some of the conceptual issues dealt with in the following chapters of this book for example, the conceptual development of anti-racist and critical race theory which have been applied to education. The conceptual debate analysed in the next chapter encompasses the first three headings when looking at the concepts of assimilation, integration and multiculturalism in terms of conservative, liberal and pluralistic notions of multiculturalism (Mirza, 2009).

Why multiculturalism and education? Why now?

As Banks and Banks highlight,

> We are living in a dangerous, confused, and troubled world that demands leaders, educators, and [needs] classroom teachers who can bridge impermeable cultural, ethnic, and religious borders, envision new possibilities, invent novel paradigms, and engage in personal transformations and visionary action. (Banks and Banks, 2007: v)

This book is an opportunity to examine why education continues to be socially and politically excluding and exclusive rather than being continually debated, multicultural and educationally inclusive.

Education needs to develop, evolve and go further, as Baker and LeTendre (2005: 2–3) highlight, when they describe education as a 'national enterprise' and a 'national technical project' which underlines a nation's culture and citizenship but fails to see global forces influencing schooling and pedagogy. Education is a global phenomena, and it is debatable where a nation state or a national curriculum can sit within a multicultural or globalized world (Lauder et al., 2006). The danger is for multiculturalism and education to get lost in debates which are vague or confusing. As Bryson suggests when reflecting on multiculturalism within the US context:

> The exact meaning is not at all clear, and mere attempts at definition can produce conflict. At its most general level, multiculturalism implies the coexistence of multiple cultures . . . the term can be applied narrowly, as in an elementary school classroom . . . and it can be applied broadly to address cultural dynamics at a global level. (Bryson, 2005: 27)

The concept of multiculturalism is far from perfect *but* the concept can be used in conjunction with the term multicultural education to analyse contemporary issues in education. As Banks and Banks remind us:

> Multicultural education is at least three things: an idea or concept, an educational reform movement, and a process. Multicultural education incorporates the idea that all students . . . should have an equal opportunity to learn in school. Another important idea in multicultural education is that some students, because of these characteristics, have a better chance to learn in schools as they are currently structured than do students who belong to other groups or who have different cultural characteristics. (Banks and Banks, 2007: 3)

The following quote is significant as it encapsulates the complexity of multiculturalism in relation to, for example, learning processes with some children having more opportunities than others because of their social and cultural background (Ball, 2003). The example of 'Being British' in a multicultural world was used on a team taught undergraduate module, *Questioning Citizenship* which is delivered at Roehampton University in London:

> Being British is about driving in a German car to an Irish pub for a Belgian beer, then travelling home, grabbing an Indian curry or a Turkish kebab on the way, to sit on Swedish furniture and watch American shows on a Japanese TV. And the most British thing of all – suspicion of anything foreign. (Woodman, 2009)

The above quote encapsulates the difficulty people the worldover have with defining their identity and questioning their citizenship. Different migrants, over different periods in history, have moved to different shores and added their different values to the cultural mix. If incoming migrants add to the cultural continuum, what do they lose within processes of social assimilation and integration? Sen (2006) informs us that ideas of identities are linked with the understanding nature and merits (or demerits) of multiculturalism. An important issue is how migrants are seen:

> Should they be categorised in terms of inherited traditions, particularly the inherited religion, of the community in which they happen to be born, taking that unchosen identity to have automatic priority over other affiliations . . . should we assess the fairness of multiculturalism primarily by the extent to which people from different cultural backgrounds are 'left alone', or by the extent to which their ability to make reasoned choices is positively supported through social opportunities of education and participation in civil society and the political and economic processes ongoing in the country? (Sen, 2006: 150)

What migrants do, either within a minority or between communities is the issue that concerns a migrant's identity. Multiculturalism is not exclusively about differences in colour, gender or class. It can also concern language and the importance of multilingualism. An example of this relates to teaching and lecturing in the English language, in non-English speaking countries, highlighting cultural issues within the internationalization of higher education. We are looking here at an application of Pierre Bourdieu's concept of cultural capital – meaning the social, political, economic and cultural resources that inform social life and situate groups apart from one another (Banks and Esposito, 2009) – whereby 'we' – defined here as practice taking part within the educational workplace – are using expertise and educational credentials to help educate students whose first language is not English (Bourdieu, 2004; 2005; Moore, 2004). By meeting the economic demand for an increase in global postgraduate qualifications, levels and standards of education theoretically increase domestically and internationally and all students benefit from educational knowledge and expertise. That goes back to what Sen (2006) is taking about earlier when he discusses people making 'reasoned choices . . . supported through social opportunities of education'. However, the issue does not simply relate to those people who can make reasoned choices by studying, but to the agents who actually deliver the education course that is, the validating institution that awards the qualification and provides the opportunity for that reasoned choice to be made in the first place. Furthermore, the issues here are not just about language and the expression of multicultures (Pathak, 2008). They are, in an educational content, about the challenges to cultural difference, student diversity (Cornbleth, 2008) student experience, and who has the ability to make and control cultural capital that defines and influences educational choice for majority and minority communities both domestically and internationally.

Reflective Exercise

- Can you apply the concept of 'cultural capital' to your educational experiences?

Contemporary issues concerning multiculturalism within education

This book seeks to increase understanding of the contemporary issues of multiculturalism in education by attempting to examine educational, social, political and conceptual factors, which controlled the evolution of multicultural education, not just in England but globally (Banks, 2009). This will be addressed in Chapter 2. In England, the publication of both the Swann Report (DES, 1985) and the MacPherson Report (HO, 1999) are two examples of official documentation that were both calling for more visible examples of cultural diversity in the taught curriculum of England and Wales. Taught subjects like citizenship currently provide statutory curricula for secondary schools and non-statutory curricula for primary schools. Citizenship theoretically provides culturally diverse opportunities for subjects like racism, terrorism and anti-discrimination to be taught (Race, 2008a; 2008b). From the literature evidence base examined for this book, education has and needs to go much further in relation to cultural diversity (Banks, 2009). Teachers need the tools and skills, taught through continuing professional development, to teach a multicultural curriculum and more significantly, survive in culturally diverse classrooms, playgrounds and staffrooms (Lieberman and Miller, 2008). Salili and Hoosain suggest multicultural education is based on several assumptions reflecting multicultural philosophy:

- The first and the most important assumption is that cultural diversity is a positive and enriching experience and helps people to learn about each other's cultures and become better and more fulfilled human beings . . . Multicultural education programs have the responsibility of reflecting the diversity of students' background in the curriculum.

- The second assumption is that 'multicultural education is for all students' and not just for minority groups. The majority group can also benefit from learning and understanding cultural differences. Hence multicultural education should be provided in all schools and not just in schools with higher minority student populations.

- The third assumption is the realization that 'teaching is a cross-cultural encounter'. Teachers and students alike have their own cultural backgrounds, values, customs, perceptions and prejudices. These cultural characteristics play an important role in teaching and learning situations and can have substantial effects on our learning and behaviour. (Salili and Hoosain, in Salili and Hoosain, 2001: 9)

It's important to highlight the second point above. Multicultural education has to be for both teachers and pupils before we can get to the 'cross-cultural encounter'. This suggests that teaching students to reflect about different cultures can allow a space for cultural understandings to increase. This is not an easy matter to address as all classrooms are educationally, socially and situationally different and will have unique and constantly changing dynamics. One of the aims of highlighting the contemporary issues of education and multiculturalism is to increase understandings of both multicultural education and practice. As Nieto and Bode correctly remark:

> When multicultural education is mentioned, many people first think of lessons in human relations and sensitivity training, units about ethnic holidays, education in inner schools, or food festivals. If multicultural education is limited to these issues, the potential for substantive change in schools is severely diminished. (Nieto and Bode, 2008: 43)

It would, for example, be impossible to have a dozen teaching assistants in a London secondary school dealing with 12 different languages spoken by pupils aged 13. Or would it? This linguistic and education issue is one of many that politicians and school leaders, at local, federal, national and international levels have to continue to address within both social and educational contexts. Senior managers, heads of department and teachers need guidance and continuing professional development opportunities to continue their education, lifelong learning and training in relation to the changing dynamics of culture and society.

Reflective Exercise

- How can cultural diversity be a contemporary, positive and enriching experience within education?
- How can teaching become more of a 'cross-cultural' encounter?

The structure of the book

In the next chapter, I address existing and ongoing conceptual debates which continue to shape how we perceive multiculturalism and other concepts that can be applied to education. This means a conceptual examination of assimilation, integration as well as multiculturalism and anti-racism. This is followed by an examination of social and policy documents that is, The MacPherson Report (HO, 1999) and Cantle Report (HO, 2001) alongside *Every Child Matters* (HO, 2003; DfES, 2004). The concepts will be applied to the policy documents to increase our understandings of cultural diversity and multiculturalism within education contexts. Chapter 3 examines Trevor Phillips' (2005) speech on Britain 'Sleepwalking to Segregation' and the question he posed, 'Is Multiculturalism Dead?' The interpretation of Phillips' arguments are significant because they allow us to focus on the political and social consequences of the concept of integration in contemporary policy contexts (Finney and Simpson, 2009). The fourth chapter addresses the issue of faith schools and multiculturalism and by looking at education policy evidence whether there is a possibility of more inclusive (DfES, 2002; DCSF, 2007) and more multi-faith schools (Flint, 2007) within an education system.

Chapter 5 examines the issues surrounding multiculturalism and education, analysing empirical evidence relating to multicultural education. One of the key issues addressed is whether the concept of multiculturalism is healthy and has a future (Eade et al., 2008). Citizenship as a concept and citizenship education as a curricula subject is highlighted as a means of producing and delivering a more culturally diverse education. These possibilities will be developed in the final chapter, alongside the need to make the teaching profession more culturally aware of diversity issues through continuing professional development (Cantle, 2008). This book will end with reflections on multicultural education and a focus on several key points which have arisen through the research process that has produced this book. The new chapter of this edition extends the citizenship debate by examining the movement from multicultural to integrationist citizenship. This continues to highlight the importance of citizenship within education but underlines the political nature of this debate. The examination of the political speeches of Merkel, Cameron and Clegg show the politics involved in debates concerning multiculturalism and education but the new reflection is to examine education policy and citizenship curricula to continue to increase understandings of how politics shapes education policy and practice. Citizenship in England and around the world continues to have multicultural opportunities and possibilities. Multicultural education needs to be continually more than an idea or a concept. If it needs to contribute, yet again, to inclusive change, then let the ongoing debates continue (Banks, 2009; Lott, 2010).

Useful websites

Citizenship and Immigration – Canada
  www.cic.gc.ca/multi/inclusv-eng.asp
Making multicultural Australia
  www.multiculturalaustralia.edu.au/
Multicultural London
  www.multicultural.co.uk/multiculturallondon.htm

Note

1. As Rmaji (2009: 17) highlights: 'It is important to recognise that race researchers will be operating with a contested category'. The contested nature of the social construction of race is addressed in a book in this series (Richards, forthcoming).

Conceptual, Social and Education Policy Background

Introduction

This chapter is a conceptual and social policy account of multicultural education. The first four sections consider conceptual debates which will put the development and evolution of multicultural education into context for the reader. Those concepts are: assimilation; integration; multiculturalism; and anti-racism. Education policies are then examined to see how these concepts shaped policy-making (DES, 1967; 1971; 1985). The focus then moves to several independent, and governmental reports which highlight social and educational responses towards multiculturalism that is, MacPherson (1999), Cantle Report (HO: 2001) and *Every Child Matters* (HO; 2003; DfES, 2004). The intention is to apply the concepts again to the policy documents with the

Table 2.1 Concepts in English Education Policy-Making Discourse (Race, 2007)

c. 1950–1965	c. 1965–1974	c. 1974–1985	c.1970s–1990s.	c. 2000–
Assimilation	Integration	Multiculturalism	Anti-Racism	Citizenship

focus concerning what consequences these policies have had for English multiculturalism and cultural diversity. The Table 2.1 will give the reader an idea of an ongoing conceptual timeframe.

Assimilation

Assimilation is an important concept to start with in relation to multicultural-ism because disturbingly, it still has contemporary application and relevance. As Modood argues:

> Assimilation is where the processes affecting the relationship between . . .
> social groups are seen as one way, and where the desired outcome for society
> as a whole is seen as involving least change in the ways of doing things of the
> majority of the country and its institutional policies. (Modood, 2007: 47–48)

Coelho (1998: 19–20) describes assimilation as '. . . a one-way process of absorption whereby minorities abandon, at least publicly, their ethnic identi-ties. An assimilationist approach regards diversity as a problem and cultural differences as socially divisive . . .'. Assimilation definitions raise the following issues. The first issue is that minority or oppressed groups are going to resist this 'one-way' process. The second issue, which is educational, concerns both children and parents and their possible resistance to school structures and the curriculum taught in the classroom. One helpful way of understanding assimilation is examining the metaphor of the melting-pot. Immigrants enter-ing the United States were encouraged to think and become American but in the process losing their original culture within the melting-pot. The aim was to develop a single American identity which shared a common culture. The image of the 'American Dream' was based on the melting-pot metaphor and therefore assimilation ideas.

Assimilationist social policies in the United Kingdom can be traced back to the 1960s. The 1962 Commonwealth Immigration Act began the process of stemming the flow of immigrants dating back to the end of the Second World War. As Cohen and Manion (1983: 18–19) highlight: 'Immigrants . . . [and] Commonwealth . . . citizens . . . were required to obtain work vouchers . . . to ensure that would-be immigrants have skills that were in current demand'. The end of a global migrant flow, not just from Commonwealth countries, forced the government to consider the social consequences of immigrants living, not just working in the United Kingdom. The issue as Tomlinson (2008: 19–43) underlines, was the need to encourage post-war immigrant labour but also devise social policies that would control the flow of immigrants while offering immigrant children an education which would provide future generations of immigrants with employment. An official education policy response to new immigrants can be seen in a government education circular published in 1971 which contained the same issues published six years before in 1965. Both education circulars were entitled 'The Education of Immigrants'. The education policy document shows how the government attempted to deal with the problems of both immigrant child and parent:

> . . . Some schools before 1960 had a cosmopolitan range of nationalities among their pupils but had found relatively little difficulty in absorbing and educating children of the earlier post-war European immigrants. In the 1960s however, the concentration and rapid build-up in the numbers of children arriving from Commonwealth countries and entering the schools at different ages and at all times throughout the school year began to create serious educational difficulties. (DES, 1971: 1)
>
> For the West Indian child . . . The environment is one in which marriage is not always considered important in providing a secure basis for raising children . . . to join his mother from whom he may have been separated for several years, almost a stranger among new unknown brothers and sisters, possibly disliking and not fully accepted by the unknown father with whom his mother may be living, and perhaps, sent out to child-minders while his parents go out to work. (DES, 1971: 4–5)
>
> Asian mothers' tendency to live a withdrawn life and not to make outside contacts does not help . . . Many (Asian parents) are shy at the thought of mixing with white parents with whom they have little or no contact out of school; some are suspicious and fear rebuffs, others are embarrassed by their inadequate command of English. (DES, 1971: 6)
>
> The education service can make its best contribution to the country's future in this situation by helping each individual immigrant to become a citizen who can take his or her place in society, fully and properly equipped to accept responsibilities, exercise rights and perform duties. (DES, 1971: 12)

What is interesting in the education policy document just outlined (see the second quote) is that the government analysis of education issues focuses on the West Indian community as the problem, not the school or the education system. The terms 'West Indian' and 'Asian' are also controversial. As Brah (in Donald and Rattansi, 1992: 126–31) argues, the term 'black' emerged to highlight the experiences of African-Caribbean and South Asian communities in post-war England. This is controversial because it was both racist and failed to acknowledge difference and cultural diversity (Gill et al., 1992). The term 'responsibilities' – which is in the fourth quote mentioned earlier – is also significant as it fails to highlight whether there is responsibility on either the citizen or on the state to help majority and minority communities within educational contexts (Race, 2001a). As Tomlinson (in Modgil et al., 1986: 12) informs us, '. . . most parents who migrated to Britain from the Caribbean and the Asian sub-continent saw success for their children as of major importance'. It is no surprise that parents would have been anxious during the 1960s as to how the English education system was treating their children. As Tomlinson (ibid.) continues, parents from minority communities were also worried about children being placed in low subject streams, remedial departments and protested to the Race Relations Board.

The evidence from the education circular mentioned earlier shows a limited understanding by the government of the culturally diverse issues the education system had been attempting to cope with during the 1950s and 1960s. New migrants and their children posed new challenges but these were viewed as new problems (Tomlinson, 2008). If the education system was perceived as a meritocratic ladder, where the opportunity for success was equal and all children could enter the competition for educational qualifications, employment and the consequent social rewards, evidence suggested that education was not open to all (Young, 1958; McCulloch in McCulloch and Crook, 2008). May (1998: 68–69) stated that 'newcomers' were initially disadvantaged by not only the unfamiliarity of the education system but the government response to this challenge which was the 'one way model of absorption'. It is claimed by Gillborn (1990) and May (1998) that this assimilationist model was ultimately to prove a failure, because Caribbean and East Asian parents mobilized and protested at a local level against assimilationist education policy. They were dissatisfied with its failure to deliver on the promise of 'meritocratic achievement for all' which would have given their children greater education and employment opportunities.

It is important to reflect on the idea of assimilation in an education context (Tomlinson, 2008) because of the loss of cultural identity when considering the melting-pot metaphor. Minority communities have no option but to change and adapt to the majority cultural identity through processes involved within an assimilationist conceptual framework. Assimilation aims to preserve the majority culture and identity. This conceptual application of assimilation may still be as relevant today as it has been in the past for all migrants.

Reflective Exercise

- Is a immigrant today prepared to abandon their identity to conform, assimilate and fit into a majority culture?
- How important is parental choice in a child's education?

Integration

Integration is defined by Modood where,

> [the] processes of social interaction are seen as two way, and where members of the majority community as well as immigrants and ethnic minorities are required to do something; so the latter cannot alone be blamed for failing (or not trying) to integrate. (Modood, 2007: 48)

Processes of social interaction and adaptation are vital for all migrants and minority communities when considering the notion of community cohesion which we will look at later in this chapter. This need to adapt focuses on the fear that immigrant children will not have the education and employment options and possibilities that were examined in the last section. It is also interesting to apply the processes of social interaction and adaptation as 'two-way' when considering relationships between majority and minority communities. The concept of integration also may be described as cultural fusion. Coelho explains that

> Cultural fusion differs from assimilation in that it involves a two-way process of adaptation and acculturation. Whereas assimilation is designed to eliminate

diversity, fusion serves to incorporate diversity in to the mainstream and, by so doing, change the mainstream. Education is an important means of creating a common cultural identity which merges majority and minority cultures. This is often referred to as *e pluribus unum* – out of many, one. (Coelho, 1998: 21)

Integration may imply a two-way process but as Modood (2007: 48) rightly argues, '. . . institutions – including employers, civil society and the government – in which integration has to take place must [accordingly] . . . take the lead'. This implies that integration, like assimilation, although being a consensual or even a conditional 'two-way' relationship, is still controlled by institutions for example, the nation state. That control is 'one-way' and as underlined in the previous chapter, cultural capital can give more advantages to some over others. And Coelho (1998) reminds us that education is a tool that creates and reinforces a 'common cultural identity'.

An important moment, which defined integration politically in England, was a speech given by the then Home Secretary, Roy Jenkins in 1966. In that speech, he defined integration as '. . . not as a flattening process of uniformity but as cultural diversity coupled with equal opportunity in an atmosphere of mutual tolerance' (Rex in Eade et al., 2008: 32). Now that in itself is an interesting political definition because it highlights the potential of integrationist policy within a *conditionally controlled, two-way* atmosphere of mutual toleration. The potential for cultural diversity is present but that notion of control by the nation state is still present. As Rex interprets, Jenkins' speech makes sense when one examines what he considers to be two cultural domains:

On the one hand it suggested a shared and unquestionable public political culture based upon equality of opportunity, on the other it allowed for the continuance in the private and communal domain of a variety of cultures based upon a diversity of languages, religious and family practices in minority communities. (Rex in Sikes and Rizvi, 1997: 110)

We can see the potential and problems with the concept of integration. The two 'cultural domains' are split between the public domain, which contains the controlling institutions as Modood (2007) explained, and the private domain which contains institutions like the family. As Rex has just suggested, the public minority are mutually tolerant of equal opportunity and cultural diversity whereas the private majority seek equal opportunity within cultural diversity. It is not a conditional relationship based on mutual tolerance. A year after the Jenkins Speech, The Plowden Report (DES: 1967) included a chapter entitled 'Children of Immigrants' which focused on among other things, the number of immigrants from 'certain' Commonwealth countries. Under the sub-heading, educational problems, some of the educational issues or problems are addressed in the following categories:

184 . . . Some special problems face local education authorities and others in areas with high concentrations of immigrants. Many immigrant children are at a disadvantage because of the poor educational background from which they have come. It is difficult to discriminate between the child who lacks intelligence and the child who is suffering from 'culture shock'; or simply from inability to communicate. As a result, few immigrant children find places in selective schools.

185 . . . Teachers have generally not been trained during their courses at colleges of education to teach immigrant children. They therefore lack knowledge of the cultural traditions and family structure that lie behind the children's concepts and behaviour. Experienced teachers of immigrant children testify that they have found it of great help to know about family tradition and habits of worship, and about food, clothing and customs, which differ from ours. Unfortunately, it is not easy to find authoritative books on these subjects suitable for teachers in training, and there has been a lack of in-service training courses.

186 . . . The next step must be the inclusion in initial training courses for some teachers, and in some refresher courses, of discussion of the background of immigrant children. Local education authorities, where there are large numbers of immigrants, could hold induction courses for new teachers in these areas.

(DES, 1967)

There are two points to take away from this education policy example. Immigrant parents and their children are again being seen as the problem, which reflects the focus of *Education of Immigrants* (DES: 1971). The solution to changing cultural diversity within education concerned the need for all groups that is, parents, children, schools, local education authorities and the government, to recognize the changing nature of society. Tomlinson (2008: 40) highlights the efforts made by some LEAs, schools and teachers to incorporate children but, '. . . the belief that their presence constituted a problem, and the lingering pseudo-scientific beliefs in the intellectual inferiority of black children also marked the [1960s]'.

Reflecting on the policy document just mentioned (DES, 1967) teachers are also not deemed to have been trained to cope with the 'problem', and the 'next steps' are for only 'some' teachers, not the whole profession to focus with dealing with cultural diversity within education. The lack of continuing professional development within education to address diverse 'cultural traditions' is clearly lacking in the 1960s. An international perspective to reflect upon at this point, as Fairclough (2007) highlights, is how the Civil Rights movement shaped education in the United States during the 1950s. Schools were promoting the concept of integration in practice with black teachers working alongside white colleagues for the first time. However, the resources for educational equal opportunity in the United States for example, black and other minority teachers, books and other materials were also lacking (Pollock, 2008). The need for more professional training using multicultural education is again acknowledged, but the implication is that this should be focused on local areas with high demographic numbers of immigrant children, rather than this being part of a federal or national development programme. As Grosvenor (1997: 56) perceptively points out concerning education policy documents in England during the 1960s and 1970s: 'Integration, as it was interpreted in policy terms, still required immigrants to make the adjustments, and while the incidence of "racial discrimination" in society at large was acknowledged, the existence of racism in education was ignored'.

The 1970s began with Margaret Thatcher, as Secretary of State at the DES (1970–1974). This period witnessed the opening of more comprehensive secondary schools than at any other time in education history in England and Wales. Significantly, the preservation of 144 grammar schools kept secondary schools divided rather than universally comprehensive (Race, 2001b). But as Tomlinson (2008: 67) reminds us, during the 1970s, an economic recession had increased the demand for education qualifications, '. . . and immigrant parents were doubly concerned that the system was not preparing their children for decent jobs or a future'. Under increasingly hard economic times in England, a Labour government was returned to power in 1974 and remained in government for five years. The years 1974 to 1985, containing both Labour and Conservative governments, were particularly important for multicultural education in England as we will examine in the next section. As the DES (1977: 4) reported, 'Ours is now a multiracial and multicultural country, and one in which traditional social patterns are breaking down'. The focus from 1974 onwards was politically, socially and educationally becoming more multicultural.

Multiculturalism

The 1970s and 1980s witnessed the application of multiculturalism and multicultural education into school policy and practice in England (DES, 1977; 1981; 1985). We have defined and examined the term multiculturalism and multicultural education in the previous chapter. As Mills (in Laden and Owen, 2007: 91–92) reminds us: 'Contemporary multiculturalism thus challenges the older hegemonic norm of *monoculturalism*, the view that non-European cultures were to a greater or lesser extent clearly inferior to European ones [and] not deserving of much or any respect . . . '. At a time when it has been mentioned that multiculturalism was been debated, the 1980s in England were marked by social disorder. Lord Scarman (1982: 26), who was responding to riots in London and Liverpool, received evidence from organizations and individuals which pointed, ' . . . to the failure of black youths to acquire sufficiently early the skills of language and literacy, and to the sense of disappointment and frustration which at least some black parents and children feel in the education system'. Scarman also acknowledged evidence obtained in the Rampton Report (DES, 1981) which reported on West Indian youth and education. The educational issues which were being addressed in policy documentation in the 1960s and 1970s in England (DES, 1967; 1971) seemed not to have changed for children from minority communities within the education system. The focus was still on the child and parent as the problem rather than the education system.

But as Mullard (in Barton and Walker, 1983: 139) recognized, the English riots in Brixton, Moss Side, Southall and Toxteth in the 1980s signified the intense resistance to ' . . . all aspects and agencies of racist authority'. 'West Indian youth' were not interested in the melting-pot or integrationist compromise. As Anthias and Yuval-Davies (1993: 158) argue, 'Multiculturalism emerged as a result of the realization, originally in the USA, and then in Britain, that the "melting-pot" doesn't melt, and that ethnic and racial divisions get reproduced from generation to generation'. West Indian communities could clearly see that cultural divisions were being reproduced (Gilroy, 2006). The term 'multicultural' was being criticized as the celebration of culture at an insubstantial level which was avoiding issues of power and oppression in society. Gundara (in Gundara et al., 1986: 11) claimed the institutions of the English state that is, local education authorities and the DES were '. . . essentially concerned with the containment of black resistance to schooling'.

However, resistance was also being expressed in black academia. As Troyna (in Troyna, 1987a: 7) acknowledges, black writers in England such as Chris Mullard, Gus John, Hazel Carby, Pratibha Parmar and Stuart Hall were reflecting '. . . the struggle against racism which members of the black community are engaged in'. A potential solution to these issues was suggested by May (1998: 30–33) who argues, '. . . the recognition of our cultural and historical situatedness should not set the limits of ethnicity and culture, nor act to undermine the legitimacy of other, equally valid forms of identity'. Thus, all communities needed to be recognized positively and not as problems. As the education policy evidence has shown, immigrant identities and cultural diversity were seen as problematic because it challenged the focus concerning the majority culture and made the debate more complex than simply achieving unity through diversity (Day, 2002). Touraine (2000: 172) adds another and slightly different definition of multiculturalism and argues it is a '. . . *meeting of cultures* . . .' which asserts the existence of cultural entities that must be respected. The issue of respecting difference theoretically takes the problem away. An educational response to these issues, especially a burgeoning acceptance and acknowledgment of 'West Indian' and 'Pakistani' children's needs came with the publication of the Swann Report (DES, 1985). As Parekh wrote:

> The English educational system in the 1980s had to address and react to a mono-cultural orientation and tradition. This was not just visible in schools, but also in what was taught and how it was taught in other areas of education e.g. universities. A multicultural curriculum would expose children and students to other societies and culture, develop imagination and critical faculties. The danger of mono-cultural education is that it '. . . breeds arrogance and insensitivity . . .' and '. . . mono-cultural education provides a fertile ground for racism'. (Parekh in Modgil et al., 1986: 22–23)

Tomlinson (1990) argued that the 1980s was an educational battleground between educational nationalism that tried to defend an education underpinned by monocultural values and was based on a myth that minorities: '. . . have complete choice and full opportunity to assimilate into the British way of life and British culture'. The other side of that battle was multicultural education.

An attempt to challenge that general myth of multiculturalism would be addressed educationally in the Swann Report of which sections are summarized in the box below:

> . . . [The Swann Report aimed to] review in relation to schools the educational needs and attainment of children from ethnic minority groups taking accounts, as necessary, of factors outside the formal education system relevant to school performance, including influences, in early childhood and prospects for school leavers. (DES, 1985: vii)
>
> [from the Rampton Report, 1981] . . . West Indian children . . . under-achieving in relation to their peers . . . no single cause . . . but rather a network of widely differing attitudes and expectations on the part of teachers and the education system as a whole, and on the part of the West Indian child to have particular difficulties and face particular hurdles in achieving his or her full potential. (DES, 1985: vii)
>
> The Report . . . Education for All . . . views the task for education in meeting the needs of ethnic minority pupils and preparing all pupils, both ethnic majority and ethnic minority, for life in a society which is both multi-racial and culturally diverse . . . (DES, 1985: xii)

What is important here is that Swann moved the problematic focus away from migrants, minority children and parents to the education system. Swann was also significant because the focus on multicultural education underlined the need to educate all children within a cultural diverse framework (Ffye in Ffye and Figueroa, 1993: 44). If we compare Swann (DES, 1985) with the two previous educational policy documents (DES, 1967; 1971) then education policy is not only recognizing but attempting to educate a culturally diverse society for the first time. Swann (DES, 1985) stressed that the education system should contribute to producing a democratic pluralistic society, which recognized all communities and offered them equal opportunities.

However, as Parekh (in Verma and Pumfrey, 1988a: 64–70) argues, the Swann Report had several limitations; in particular, the continuation of negative stereotypes towards the terms being used in the 1980s that concerned West Indian and Asian families. It was not only 'West Indian' and 'Asian' Families that were disadvantaged. As Tomlinson (2008: 93) suggests, 'More understanding of the origins and values underpinning the curriculum was required rather than arguing about the content of subjects'.

When considering other international perspectives during the mid-1980s, Taylor (1987: 289–90) examines how English skills through the teaching of English as a second language meant that less attention was paid to elements of Chinese culture and language for pupils of Chinese origin. Swann acknowledged China as being a 'world civilization' but it was as important for '. . . businessman and industrialists to know more about the economic importance of Hong Kong'. Taylor (1988) also underlined little evidence in education research for Cypriots and teachers' awareness of the cultural needs of children from Cyprus. Negative stereotypes of Chinese and Cypriot communities could only be overcome with the creation a more culturally diverse curriculum.

Swann (DES, 1985) also failed to clarify what it actually meant when it mentioned the term pluralism. As Coelho highlights, cultural pluralism, often referred to as multiculturalism,

> . . . involves creating a cohesive society where individuals of all backgrounds interact and participate equally, while maintaining their cultural identities. Unlike other conceptual approaches, like assimilation, which essentially views diversity issues as a problem, multiculturalism views diversity as an asset. (Coelho, 1998: 21)

Interestingly, this concept of cultural pluralism had been developed in Canada (see the previous chapter) where the metaphors of the 'multicultural mosaic' and 'salad bowl' had been devised to signify a combination of identities and a positive focus on cultural diversity (Day, 2002; Robinson, 2007). Conceptually, these metaphors were more pluralistic and multicultural than the assimilationist 'melting-pot'. This use of the Canadian metaphors could have gone a long way in raising awareness of multiculturalism when the education system in England and Wales during the 1980s needed to change to acknowledge fluid and diverse cultures (CDSoS, 1987; CMoSMC, 1991). Yet as Tomlinson (2008: 97) points out, the problems of acceptance and recognition were different in England than in Canada: 'Intense conflict surrounded the acceptance of former colonial immigrants and their children, now recognized in law as Black and Asian citizens or potential citizens'.

Swann (DES, 1985) did however underline the issue of 'lifestyle and values systems'. The plurality of that statement is significant as cultural diversity seemed to be a concern alongside law and order that is, social unity (Figueroa, 1991). The focus seemed to remain on the traditional, British lifestyle and value system. As Gillborn (in Majors, 2001: 15) argues, the '. . . rhetoric of cultural pluralism, remained just that, rhetoric with diversity and tolerance being discussed and debated, receiving official recognition in the Swann Report, but not filtering down into schools and staffrooms'. Gillborn (ibid.) was critical of the Rampton / Swann analysis as were the Conservative governments of the 1980s, who rejected the most important recommendations and barely mentioned the term 'racism'. Even though Swann produced evidence of a swing away from an assimilation and integration towards multicultural education policy, English education, in some cases remained the same.

So, what was the legacy of Swann (DES, 1985)? As Verma (Verma et al., 2007: 23–24) acknowledges, 'Swann . . . was the product of a widely recognized need for social justice and for equality of opportunity'. However, there was still much missing from the publication of the Swann Report. It has to be remembered that the education policy document was published by a Conservative government and the period from 1985 to the publication of the Education Reform Act (DES, 1988) has been described in this context by Troyna (1993: 75–78) as 'the conservative restoration'. The promotion of a multicultural curriculum remained after the publication of the Swann Report. However, as Singh (1993: 9–10) argues, '. . . the tokenistic inclusion of Black Studies, Asian Studies and Ethnic Studies needed to go much further to promote more than a harmonious and "well-integrated" society'. The term 'integrated' is used here which implies that Swann's legacy did not provide the space nor incentive for a multicultural curriculum to be produced. What was required, in the spirit of Swann (DES, 1985) during the late 1980s and 1990s was both a recognition and celebration of difference (Jenkins, 1997). What the Conservative governments in England and Wales produced in education was a 'national' curriculum of three core and seven foundation subjects (Race, 2001a). The 'lifestyle and values systems' would, as Anthias and Yuval-Davies (1993: 184–85) argue, become problematic if minority issues in education were oversimplified.

In the United States, during the 1980s, multicultural education was highlighted by Banks (in Fyfe and Figueroa, 1993) as being dominated by budget cuts in social programmes meaning that education programmes would be frozen or cut. Weil not only suggests what is required, but also what needs to be avoided as:

> Multicultural approaches to education that encourage self-examination, self-awareness, cultural critiques and personal growth through an identification with and an understanding of one's own culture or heritage represent an authentic pedagogical movement toward egalitarianism and human

fair-mindedness in educational discourse and action. On the other hand, inculcating a view of the world from only one cultural point of view promotes sophisticated narrow-minded thinking and is pedagogically dishonest. (Weil, 1998: 15–17)

> ## Reflective Exercise
>
> - How do the metaphors of the 'melting-pot', the 'mosaic' and the 'salad bowl' help us increase our understandings of multiculturalism?
> - What were the positive and negative factors of the Swann Report (DES,1985)?

Anti-racism

It is worth examining the anti-racist approach which was critical of multiculturalism in England during the 1970s and 1980s. For Gundara (1986: 11–12): 'Anti-racism both specifies a key element in the analysis of British society in that racism is embedded in our interpersonal relations, in our ideology and in our institutions, and also adopts a moral and political stance towards it'. In a different context, 'anti-racism was developed by Black Power movements in the USA which opposed both the melting-pot metaphor of assimilation but also more contemporary multicultural approaches' (Anthias and Yuval-Davies, 1993). Sewell's analysis goes further when focusing on both multicultural and anti-racist policy:

> Too many multicultural and antiracist policies are tokenistic documents which no one owns. There is a need to probe the silence and get behind the policy text. In many cases, schools are embarrassed about even making reference to anti-racism. They may adopt a more strident tone over issues like sex discrimination and bullying but still become opaque when it comes to the vexed issue of race and racism. (Sewell's, 2000: 189–90)

However, the anti-racist concept does go further than multiculturalism when looking for the conditions to produce social equity and equal opportunities, thereby addressing racism within education (Troyna, 1992; Race, 2009a). The anti-racist approach examines systems which control schooling and access to the curriculum which offers more life chances to some groups over others. For Dei (in Dei and Johal, 2005: 3), anti-racism is about power relations: 'It sees race and racism as central to how we claim, occupy and defend spaces. The task of anti-racism is to identify, challenge and change the structures, and behaviours that perpetuate systemic racism and other forms of societal oppression'.

Troyna (1987b; 1992; 1993; 1998; Troyna and Williams, 1986) was the main advocate of the anti-racist position in England. Unsurprisingly, he attacks the Swann Report for its multicultural position and failing to address the issue of providing anti-racist education in multi-racist Britain. As Troyna argued (in Chivers, 1987b: 39–40), Swann created 'superficial changes' to the structure of the education system and provided little support for those who argued for anti-racist changes for education. These changes, as Troyna (ibid.) continued, were created by those, '. . . committed to "cultural tourism" of the three Ss (Saris, Samosas and Steel Bands) conception of educational change'. Troyna highlighted the weaknesses of multiculturalism and the advantages of anti-racism (Race, 2009a).

Anti-racism as a concept challenged the Conservative education policy of the 1980s and 1990s which endorsed some of Swann's recommendations. What is significant in the educational research that Troyna carried out in the 1970s and 1980s was that teachers would cope with the issues of culturally diverse classrooms, and the complexity of these social arenas went far beyond the metaphor of the multicultural salad bowl. For anti-racists like Troyna (in Gill et al., 1992: 63), race related social and educational policy was needed '. . . as an immediate and pragmatic strategy for teachers to cope with the day to day reality of their work'. Troyna (1992) implied that researchers should theoretically come from all communities to collect empirical data on educational issues that concern racism because it is this diversity of interpretation concerning all communities which is needed in society (Troyna and Williams, 1986: Steinberg, 2009).

From an anti-racist position, what is important to note is that the dominant discourse which was politically active in England and Wales from 1985 onwards, a conservative multiculturalism, failed to build on existing multicultural practice in schools (Troyna, 1993; 1995). The anti-racist position was an alternative to this and as Reed (in Griffiths and Troyna, 1995: 94) argued, teachers should have been more active and 'committed' in promoting community and producing a more anti-racist, radical agenda. This would become increasingly difficult as the 'privatisation of education' (Ball, 2007) continued into the 1990s and into the new century.

Gillborn (2008a) argues, New Labour failed to move beyond a superficial notion of equal opportunities in the first decade of the twenty-first century.

He also suggests New Labour also failed to get near an anti-racist or a Critical Race Theory (CRT) approach in relation to social justice, nor education policies which attempted to address racist educational inequality. The notion of CRT, which is examined in more depth in Chapter 6, is described by Gillborn (2008a: 27–31) as a focus on racism and critiquing liberalism through a storytelling and counter storytelling methodology. In relation to racist educational inequality, Ball highlights when examining DfES statistics from 2005:

> the data suggest that experience of and engagement with school is very often different for students of different ethnicities. In particular for black Caribbean students and, more especially, black Caribbean boys, historic patterns of underachievement, exclusion and labelling remain entrenched despite some recent improvements in participation and performance. (Ball, 2008: 167)

It seems from the evidence that Ball examines that the conceptual and education policies used to encourage multiculturalism and anti-racism in England had not produced the desired outcomes. It is therefore clear that issues of conflict and resolution that concern all teachers and students in multicultural and anti-racist contexts still need to be researched, debated and addressed (Race, 2009a).

Reflective Exercise

- How important are the concepts of anti-racism and multiculturalism today within education?

The MacPherson Report

It is important to reflect on the MacPherson Report (1999) of the death of Stephen Lawrence when considering anti-racism (Brooks, 2003). The report highlighted as Gallagher (2004: 100–01) underlines, '. . . an extraordinary lack of action and concern by the police authorities in investigating the murder of Stephen Lawrence (in South East London in 1993) and attributed this to "institutional racism" within the police service'. The aim here is not a focused debate on institutional racism (Parsons, 2008) although it should be remembered that the Scarman Report (1982) into the inner city riots in London and Liverpool had a great deal of evidence which implied institutional racism among the two police forces in the early 1980s. The MacPherson Report was different to the Scarman Report in the sense that the concept of institutional racism was actually defined but the MacPherson Report also included specific recommendations for education and how education could be used to prevent extreme situations by encouraging a positive promotion of cultural diversity within education. The education recommendations from the report are in the box below:

Prevention and the Role of Education

67. *That consideration be given to amendment of the National Curriculum aimed at valuing cultural diversity and preventing racism, in order better to reflect the needs of a diverse society.*
68. *That Local Education Authorities and school governors have the duty to create and implement strategies in their schools to prevent and address racism. Such strategies to include:*
    - *that schools record all racist incidents;*
    - *that all recorded incidents are reported to the pupils' parents/guardians, school governors and LEAs;*
    - *that the numbers of racist incidents are published annually, on a school by school basis; and*
    - *that the numbers and self defined ethnic identity of 'excluded' pupils are published annually on a school by school basis.*
69. *That OFSTED inspections include examination of the implementation of such strategies.*
    (Recommendations from the Stephen Lawrence Inquiry, Home Office (1999))

Recommendation 67 is very important here because you can see how far the education policy process has moved from the Swann Report (DES, 1985). The MacPherson recommendation is calling for changes within the national curriculum that not only 'values' cultural diversity but also aims to prevent racism. Now that interpretation encompasses what anti-racists like Troyna (1992; 1993) called for in the 1970s and 1980s. The MacPherson Report (1999) also placed responsibility on LEAs and school governors to implement anti-racist school policies and the education Inspectorate were supposed to examine if the school and local authorities were implementing these education policies. In educational terms, the MacPherson report highlights how education could be theoretically and practically used to prevent racism within education institutions and how the curriculum needed to change to reflect changing cultural diversity. However, as Gillborn (2008a: 128) points out, the above recommendations, '. . . did nothing to advance anti-racist education: it simply provided for basic civic lessons and institutionalized a weak understanding of discrimination that is entirely at odds with the thrust of the Lawrence Inquiry'. Citizenship would be added to the national curriculum in 2002, which could provide the statutory and non-statutory curriculum to teach civic lessons. The potential of the citizenship curriculum will be analysed in the final chapter of this book.

The Cantle Report

The Cantle Report (HO, 2001) published an independent report into the inner city disturbances that occurred in cities and towns in the north of England in 2001. The review team was chaired by Ted Cantle and the terms of reference were partly: '*To obtain the views of local communities, including young people, local authorities, voluntary and faith organisations, in a number of representative multi-ethnic communities, on the issues that need to be addressed in developing confident, active communities and social cohesion*' (HO, 2001: 5 emphasis in the original). Cantle and his team addressed issues such as physical segregation on housing estates and the level of social polarization in towns and cities that had been involved in the riots. The major concept that the review team created was community cohesion (Cantle, 2008) which called for amongst many things, local partnerships between communities. The analysis here focuses not only what the review had to say about education but also what was written on integration and segregation in order to increase understanding of how these ideas can be applied but obstruct debates relating to communities:

> These concepts are often posed as alternatives and can therefore hinder a sensible debate. In fact, there are many different layers which need to be separated and considered. For example, communities can often be divided into distinct housing areas and many schools (including the existing faith schools – mainly Christian) can appear to foster separation. (HO, 2001: 28)

Segregation is being implied with housing, education and faith fostering social and physical separation. Integration has already been shown to analyse how a two-way view of cultural diversity can be considered and applied

(Modood, 2007). But this quote describes 'many different layers' which need to be considered and the implied social and cultural pluralities. However, these layers are divided. This certainly resonates with Trevor Phillips and his speech where he argued that Britain was 'Sleepwalking to Segregation'. His speech will be examined in the next chapter. The Home Office Report highlighted several issues, the first relating to what the review describes as 'mono cultural schools' and community cohesion:

> In terms of community cohesion, however, a significant problem is posed by existing and future mono-cultural schools, which can add significantly to the separation of communities described above. The development of more faith-based schools may, in some cases, lead to an increase in mono-cultural schools but the problem is not in any way confined to them. We believe that all schools owe a responsibility to their pupils to promote, expand and enrich their experiences, by developing contacts with other cultures . . . or by ensuring that, as far as possible, they are represented within the school intake. Contact with other cultures should be a clear requirement for, and development of, the concept of citizenship education from September 2002 – and possibly a condition for funding. This should be seen as a demanding responsibility. (HO, 2001: 33)

Segregation and separation are being discussed by Cantle, but the cause of community division is perceived as partly educational with faith based and monocultural schools. Education is also perceived in the above quote as a site, as it was in the MacPherson Report (1999), to promote cultural diversity. The education subject of citizenship, which was introduced a year after the publication of the Cantle Report, is deemed as the means where 'contact with other cultures' should be a clear requirement for citizenship curriculum. The Home Office Report continues:

> We therefore, propose that all schools – whether faith or non-faith based – should seek to limit their intake from one culture or ethnicity. They should offer, at least 25% of places to reflect the other cultures or ethnicities within the local area. We recognise that it is difficult to discriminate on the grounds of culture or ethnicity (the latter would be subject to legal challenge) and, in any event, the school may be less attractive to parents and children from the cultures. Indeed, the local culture or ethnicity may be the same as that of the predominant culture of the school. (ibid.)

The 25 per cent figure is a recommendation to turn monocultural schools into more multicultural schools but you can see the legal difficulties which the review team recognize in doing this. Schools could legally object to this measure if necessary. The report, however, recognizes that many people expressed views about issues concerning segregation and monocultural schools, including those which were faith based. The report also recognized the need to be as fair and equitable to Muslim and other faith communities, as Christian schools were already being partly or fully supported by state funding. This issue will be raised again in Chapter 4 when the education policy response to faith schooling in England is examined (DfEE, 2001; DfES, 2002). The review team highlight the problems of monocultural schools in the box below.

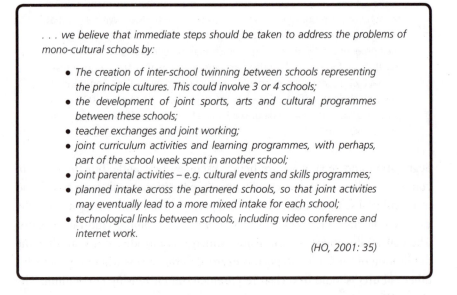

. . . we believe that immediate steps should be taken to address the problems of mono-cultural schools by:

- The creation of inter-school twinning between schools representing the principle cultures. This could involve 3 or 4 schools;
- the development of joint sports, arts and cultural programmes between these schools;
- teacher exchanges and joint working;
- joint curriculum activities and learning programmes, with perhaps, part of the school week spent in another school;
- joint parental activities – e.g. cultural events and skills programmes;
- planned intake across the partnered schools, so that joint activities may eventually lead to a more mixed intake for each school;
- technological links between schools, including video conference and internet work.

(HO, 2001: 35)

It is significant that the focus here is on the problems of monocultural schools which imply that more educational cultural recognition is required within schools and the curriculum. 'Inter-school' twinning however does not mention different cultures, only 'principle cultures', so the problem here is that less successful schools, whatever their cultural composition, could be excluded from these potential collaborations. Teacher exchanges and joint working is an interesting idea which could theoretically give members of the profession a greater understanding of what is involved in different, multicultural environments. More parental responsibility in education is implied or perhaps a social partnership with schools is a future possibility. However, this is not defined and some parents may be in a better position than others to give time to their children and local school or community. Planned or mixed intakes is also an interesting idea, 25 per cent being the recommended figure that monocultural schools should consider. In the context of monocultural schools, let us now examine recommendations from the Cantle Report that were specifically educational in their scope:

Education Recommendations of the Cantle Report

All schools should be under a statutory duty to promote a respect for, and an understanding of, the cultures in the school and neighbouring areas, through a programme of cross-cultural contact. This could be an expansion of the introduction of citizenship education from September 2002. Schools should not be afraid to discuss difficult areas and the young people we met wanted to have this opportunity and should be given a safe environment in which to do so.

All schools should ensure that, in teaching programmes and their daily activities, they respect the needs of different faiths and cultures that make up the school . . .

The recruitment of ethnic minority teachers and governors also requires review, as does diversity training for all staff and governors . . .

(HO, 2001: 36–37)

The promotion and understanding of cultures can only take place if cultural diversity is actually taught in schools. The promise and potential of the new citizenship curriculum which would be introduced a year after the publication of The Home Office report is visible in the first bullet point in the above box. A review of continuing professional development is also relevant with the recommendation of targeting not only ethnic minority but all teachers concerning practice in all schools. This highlights what was recommended in the Swann Report (DES, 1985) and is a massive education policy leap from the 1970s (DES, 1971) in both attitude and application towards cultural diversity and recognition of minority communities in education.

But what is not recognized is the wider social picture. Back (in Knowles, C. and Alexander, C., 2005: 19) acknowledges: 'Beneath the sign of places names like "Brixton" or "Handsworth" or "Southall" [in England] are racial coded landscapes created as exotic or dangerous by turns that act like a kind of A–Z of racist geography'. It is that knowledge of the complexity of the social and consequent cultural landscape that makes the implementation of [education] policy possible. When reflecting on anti-racism the need for a focus on racism within communities was also an important omission from the Cantle Report when considering social, cultural and education issues.

Every Child Matters

It is always better to prevent failure than tackle a crisis later

(DCSF, 2007)

Every Child Matters (HO, 2003) importance as a policy document resides not only in the government's reaction to the deaths of Victoria Climbie, Jasmine Beckford, Lauren Wright and Aimee Walker, but also to the Department for Education and Skills' reaction to the Home Office proposals (DfES, 2004). *Every Child Matters* (HO: 2003) called for more joined-up government intervention into child care and quicker reactions to individual child cases which instigated a stronger 'sense of accountability'. Another interesting notion in the context of this chapter within *Every Child Matters* (HO: 2003) was one of 'accountability and integration'. The concept of integration has already been examined in this chapter with a two-way relationship being applied to child care in this context (Modood, 2007). The notion of accountability is significant because *who* is actually accountable is the issue here. Joined-up government is nothing new, the police, social services and teachers have all been involved in child care issues long before 2003. The Home Office paper called for a new Minister for Children, Young People and Families in the then Department for Education and Skills. The policy document would also remove the word education and replace it with the word children from a department dealing with the education system that is, the Department for Children, Schools and Families.

Let us return to the term 'accountability and integration'. Key services, it was argued should be

> integrated within a single organisational focus . . . and a new Director of Children's Services should be created who would be accountable for local education authorities and children's social services, alongside the new Minister for Children, Young People and Families. (HO, 2003: 9)

It has been noted earlier in this chapter how integration as a social and educational concept can be perceived as a conditional, two-way relationship which can be controlled by the state rather than theoretically being mutually beneficial for everyone. It has also been noted that education policy documents of the 1960s and early 1970s focused on the child and parent as the problem rather than the education system itself. This problematic focus is again visible in *Every Child Matters* (HO: 2003). The following casual links concerning children and social problems were also highlighted in *Every Child Matters*:

- Low income and parental unemployment;
- homelessness;
- poor parenting;
- poor schooling;
- post-natal depression among mothers;
- low birth weight;
- substance misuse;
- individual characteristics such as intelligence;
- community factors, such as living in a disadvantaged neighbourhood. (HO, 2003: 17)

Everybody seems to be being blamed here but the word 'parent' is mentioned twice in the list of bullet points. This education policy focus on the parent and child as the problem rather than the state or system of child care is unfortunately visible again, as it was in the analysis of education policy documentation of the 1960s and 1970s. It is also significant in the final bullet point above and reflecting on the Cantle Report (HO:2001), that community factors were still an issue, two years after the introduction of the concept of community cohesion had been debated and theoretically applied in disadvantaged neighbourhoods in England. Cultural diversity and multiculturalism, as well as the new citizenship curriculum are also terms missing from this policy document. The omission of the citizenship curriculum, when considering joined-up government is strange as teachers and schools and the potential of a new curriculum subject can be seen as a crucial part of an evolving outlook on 'joined-up government'.
Poor schooling is also identified as being a casual link with general social problems, the need for a new Director of Children's Service and the new Minister being a governmental attempt to produce more effective social services through accountability and integration. It was also claimed ' . . . that the existing system

for supporting children and young people who are beginning to experience difficulties is often poorly co-ordinated and accountability is unclear' (HO: 2003: 21). Assessment for child care, it was argued, in some cases led to inconsistent, if any, support for children and in extreme cases for example, Victoria Climbie, led to extreme consequences (HO, 2003; DfES, 2004).

Reflective Exercise based on consultation questions from *Every Child Matters* (HO, 2003: 80)

- How can we encourage better integration of funding for supporting services for children and young people?
- Can young people be involved in local decision making and should the Government establish minimum standards for this?

The DfES (2004) response to *Every Child Matters* (HO, 2003) is important to highlight because the document gives us an education response to the government's policy. The objective of *Every Child Matters* (HO, 2003) was for every child to fulfil their potential, regardless of their background or circumstances. Again, 'background and circumstances' are significant here in what is missing as there is no mention of diversity or cultural diversity and how this may affect a child fulfilling her / his potential. Integrating services was also more specially examined in an educational context within this policy response to *Every Child Matters* (HO, 2003). As the DfES (2004) states, '. . . more effective support for pupils with complex needs will require multi-agency support'. Two common processes that should make this easier are:

- A Common Assessment Framework to help schools identity when a pupil's needs can be met within the school and to enable better targeted referral to other specialist services when needed so they can respond more effectively.
- Cross-government guidance on information-sharing to improve the sharing of information between schools and other agencies about individual children with additional needs. In time, this is likely to be supported by new databases or indexes containing basic information about each child or young person that will enable schools to make contact more easily with other practitioners involved. (DfES, 2004: 3)

Accountability, when considering 'integration and accountability', can be seen for all children in the Common Assessment Framework and the sharing of information should theoretically meet the 'background and circumstances' relating to children's needs. The DfES attempted to ensure that all children should: 'Be safe; enjoy and achieve; make a positive contribution and achieve economic well-being . . .' (2004: 1). It has to be stated that there is absolutely no focus or mention of cultural diversity in these policy documents (HO, 2003; DfES, 2004) which needs to be recognized within a joined-up government focus on children from all backgrounds and cultures needing to be local, regional and national.

Reflective Exercise

- In what ways does *Every Child Matter* (HO, 2003; DfES, 2004) today?
- What are the consequences of education being made more accountable and all social services, including education, having to integrate to improve?

Summary

This chapter has conceptually analysed the development of multiculturalism and education by highlighting social and education policy documents with governmental reports. Conceptually, a path has been followed whereby education policy documents in England and Wales were shaped by assimilation and integration ideas (DES, 1967; DES, 1971). This changed with the Swann Report (DES: 1985) with an attempt to apply multicultural ideas to education. This was criticized by both multiculturalists and anti-racists who argued that Swann (DES, 1985) did not go far enough. The 'melting-pot', 'mosaic' and 'salad bowl' metaphors were just that, images that had little application to the social and cultural realities. The debate has moved on beyond the multicultural metaphors of the 1970s, 1980s and 1990s (Millington et al., 2008; Levine-Rasky and Ringrose, 2009).

The policy debate in England begins to change with first, a call for more culturally diverse values in the education curriculum away from assimilation and integration ideas (MacPherson, 1999). However, we see a conceptual backward step away from multiculturalism and anti-racism towards integration and with the call for 'community cohesion' (HO: 2001) and the need for 'integration and accountability' in relation to children's care and their education (HO: 2003; DfES, 2004). That is the conceptual and education policy warning of this chapter. Conceptually, it is a disadvantage to go backwards with ideas when considering the two-way integrationist social relationship which is conditional and controlled by the state. A multicultural and anti-racist education (Race, 2009a) offers more for a changing and diverse population than an integrationist inspired curriculum that has in the past blamed both parents and children as causes of education problems. The idea of a conceptual reversal away from multiculturalism and back to integration needs to be examined and in the next chapter we will do that when analysing what Trevor Phillips (2005) said in relation to the death of multiculturalism and 'Britain Sleepwalking to Segregation'.

Useful websites

Black History Month
   www.black-history-month.co.uk/
Community Cohesion: A Report of the Independent Review Team
   http://image.guardian.co.uk/sys-files/Guardian/documents/2001/12/11/co mmunitycohesionreport.
   pdf
Every Child Matters
   www.dcsf.gov.uk/everychildmatters/
The MacPherson Report into the Stephen Lawrence Inquiry
   www.archive.official-documents.co.uk/document/cm42/4262/sli-00.htm
The Swann Report– 'Education for All' (DES, 1985)
   www.dg.dial.pipex.com/documents/docs3/swann.shtml

Is Multiculturalism Dead? Was Britain 'Sleepwalking to Segregation'?

Chapter Outline

Introduction

This chapter focuses on a speech made by the then Chairperson of the Commission for Racial Equality (CRE), Trevor Phillips, entitled *After 7/7: Sleepwalking to Segregation*. It is also a response to that speech and the questions that it raised in relation to multiculturalism and education. Phillips' (2005) speech was controversial in the sense that he addressed difficult social and cultural questions shortly after the 7/7 terrorist attacks on London (Eade et al., 2008; Race, 2008b; Race, 2008c; Finney and Simpson, 2009: 94–95). Phillips engaged with the conceptual debate concerning assimilation, integration and multiculturalism. By using the United States as an example, he examined the controversial subject of segregation and warned of the dangers of greater British cultural and social segregation. The context of integrationist education and social policy has already been discussed in the previous chapter but that focus continues with the issue of segregation and the consequences this has had on integrationist and multiculturalist ideas. By examining Phillips' (2005) speech in depth in relation to the two questions posed in the chapter title, the aim is to underline the need to continue to debate the causes and consequences of segregation, integration and multiculturalism.

7/7 – the age of risk and terror

The timing of Trevor Phillips' speech is significant as it occurred shortly after the July 2005 terrorist attacks (the 7th and 21st) on London. The speech has to be seen as a reaction to extreme events (Tullock, 2006; Hicks, 2007). Bhavani et al. (2005) acknowledge how debates surrounding terror are controlled by politicians and the media, who they claim, incite racial hatred rather than examine the causes of the social issues which led to terrorist attacks. This echoes some of the findings of the Cantle Report (HO: 2001) into the civic disturbances in northern English cities when calling for greater community cohesion which was explored in the previous chapter. Bhavani et al. (2005: 48) also suggest that debates surrounding issues of racism and community cohesion should be questioned and the focus should reside elsewhere, namely in forums outside of the media and politics whereby: '. . . there is a need to continuously explore the changing nature of racism as it manifests itself in our British towns against the backdrop of an uncertain globalizing world'.

In this context, Trevor Phillips is measured in his initial response to the aftermath of the 7/7 terrorist attacks, highlighting the role of the then Centre for Racial Equality in England:

> In the weeks following 7/7, [the CRE] Commission personnel and more importantly, the thousands of folk we support in communities around the country, were concentrating on . . . crucial tasks:
>
> - Encouraging communities to come forward with information that would help us tackle the threat of terrorism;
> - reassuring communities from which the perpetrators of the 7/7 and 21/7 outrages came, that they should not be the targets of scapegoats of retribution; and combating the divisions that these events threatened to open up within communities, and preventing those who would exploit those divisions for racist or Islamophobic purposes from doing so. (Phillips, 2005: 1)

The second bullet point is particularly interesting as the claim being made concerns the issue that Muslim communities towards the end of 2005 should not be made the 'targets or scapegoats of retribution' by communities, the press and politicians, even though they should be encouraged to come forward with information relating to local communities and terrorist activity. The aim of information gathering was theoretically to prevent social division, promoting community cohesion and examining the causes relating to why extreme events such as 7/7 took place. Government policy, as well as social reactions in differ-ent cultural communities in Britain, during the first decade of the twenty-first century, had been influenced by military interventions in Afghanistan and Iraq. The biggest peace time demonstration in British history took place in London protesting against military involvement on 15 February 2003 which concerned the existence of weapons of mass destruction in Iraq. Sen (2006: 151) highlights an example of the French newspaper *Le Monde* publishing an article six weeks after the 7/7 terrorist attack entitled 'The British Multicultural Model in Crisis' which suggests there was something inherently wrong with the concept of multiculturalism in Britain. The newspaper headline is signifi-cant if you consider any dictionary translation of 'crisis', which is defined as the need to make a 'choice'. The choice here revolves around a debate concerning the future of multiculturalism. Sen also acknowledges the defensive response from the United States in relation to generally 'the war on terror' and specifi-cally terrorist attacks by James Goldston when he argues:

> Don't use the very real threat of terrorism to justify shelving more than a quarter century of British achievement in the field of race relations . . . I will argue that the real issue is not whether [multiculturalism] has gone too far, . . . but what particular form multiculturalism should take. Is multiculturalism nothing other than the tolerance of diversity of cultures? Does it make a dif-ference who chooses the cultural practices, whether they are imposed in the name of 'the culture of the community' or whether they are freely chosen by persons with adequate opportunity to learn about alternatives? What facili-ties do members of different communities have, in schools as well as in the society at large, to learn about the faiths – and non-faiths – of different people in the world and to understand how to reason about choices that human beings must, if only implicitly make? (Sen, 2006: 151–52)

Sen suggests that multiculturalism is a concept that has to be recognized and evidence of past good work concerning race relations in Britain is clearly visible. Sen also suggests that the positive side of multiculturalism should not be neglected and shaped by extreme events such as terrorist attacks. Free choice is significant for all cultures here because it does matter who chooses, influences and shapes cultural practice. However, the issue of 'free choice' when people choose their cultural practices is reduced when a controlled 'two-way' integrationist process is involved. Sen also implies that free choice can be shaped in faith and non-faith schools in relation to understanding how to reason. What is significant within the issues raised by Sen in this chapter is that debates concerning multiculturalism are ongoing and are perhaps as or more significant after the 7/7 bombings on London than before (Eade et al., 2008).

Reflective Exercise

- Was 7/7 the first terrorist attack on mainland Britain? Could it happen again?

Terrorism, cultural diversity and education

Race (in Eade et al., 2008: 1–7) highlighted that three of the four terrorist attackers on London on 7 July 2005 were educated to further or higher levels of education in England. In relation to ongoing research on this theme, Bloom (2008) raised the following question from a conference paper given on multiculturalism and education (Race, 2008b): 'Can teaching diversity prevent terrorism' (Race, 2008c)? The empirical data collected from several interviewees: a university teacher trainer; a postgraduate student; a teacher trainee's comment in a questionnaire; and, another teacher trainer gives both more context to Phillips (2005) speech but also has important implications for issues examined in this book concerning multiculturalism and education:

- *University Teacher Trainer (1) – I don't think teaching diversity would stop people being recruited. It wouldn't do that. What I think teaching diversity could do is encourage a plural way of thinking. . . . We have to see it in a wider, historical perspective and understand that the terror threat that we face now is lower now than what we faced in the 1980s. I don't think it is in the power of schools to prevent people being recruited into terrorist cells. I don't think that can happen.*

- *Postgraduate Student – Terrorism will happen whatever you try and do. There are those who are sucked in by the so-called fundamentalists and they in effect are brainwashed. No matter what you do, you will have terrorism.*
- *Teacher Trainee – Well, there are two basic reasons. One is that to say, I'm dominant, part of the dominant group in this country. If I understand the other that little bit better then I'm going to be less likely to treat them as the other . . . there is not an us and them. We are all together, we understand each other. And the other thing of course is that they are also going to learn about my culture and whatever my culture is and the differences within the dominant culture of Britain . . . So, it is getting people to see that some of their prejudices and assumptions can be questioned, from both sides of an argument.*
- *University Teacher Trainer (2) – [When] teaching diversity . . . you could get into a lot of assumptions about who is different . . . it comes back to my point of hybridised, second and third generation identities when many of these kids feel alienated from their 'home culture', and have created new, different identities and it's these new identities that I think we need to be interested in . . . in terms of moving this debate forward. . . . I think it is a question of how that teaching will manifest in classrooms. What I think in terms of why, in terms of 7/7 and the hostility that is sometimes emerging between different minority ethic groups or religious groupings, as is currently the case, is that it can usually be traced back to feelings of great injustice and obviously you've got racism, you've got Islamophobia which are driving people into their isolated communities or religious theology . . . and injustices like the war, which has had a massive impact on radicalising young Islamic youth. So to me, it is those . . . I'm talking about injustice in terms of poverty and racism and our foreign policy. To my mind, it is injustice [and] racism that is the root of these problems.*

Reflecting on the variety of issues relating to whether teaching cultural diversity can prevent terrorism, the university teacher trainer (1) and the postgraduate student talk about recruitment into terror cells which in their opinions, schools can do little to prevent. The teacher trainee implies that education and therefore teaching cultural diversity can be used to question stereotypes and prejudice, although the university teacher trainer (2) warns against the dangers of assumptions of difference and 'accentuating the difference'. The university teacher trainer (2) also underlines, like Bhavani et al. (2005) that the issue that needs to be addressed is racism, alongside poverty and foreign policy in debates concerning multiculturalism. The debates in schools therefore need to be wide ranging and go beyond terror and cultural diversity. Another theme which arose from others respondents within both interviews and questionnaires was the potential of education, and especially the citizenship curriculum which has the potential to highlight not only issues of terror and cultural diversity, but debate subjects like racism and poverty.

Reflective Exercise

- Should subjects like extremism and terrorism be taught or / and discussed in classrooms and lecture theatres?

The continuing dangers of social and cultural segregation

Before we analyse what Phillips (2005) meant by 'Sleepwalking to Segregation', it is useful to show how segregation is defined. Phillips was using the United States as an example of a country which was segregated along colour and cultural lines. Cantle provides us with clearer understanding of how the term segregation is used within an English context:

> The literal meaning suggests a separation of particular groups, which is decreed by law and enforced by the state, or created by the presence of such significant barriers that the ability to move to other areas cannot be freely exercised and is 'involuntary'. However, 'segregation' has become more generally used to denote an area, which is dominated by one group [which becomes] effectively mono-cultural. The term 'self-segregation' has also been employed to describe this process, where it is assumed that particular communities have preferred to live in separate areas – in other words, the segregation is 'voluntary' (although such assumptions often overstate the real constraints upon free choice). However, whatever the cause of 'segregation' the impact on inter-community relations is profound and the lack of contact between communities can lead to ignorance and irrational fears of each other, especially where extremists seek to capitalise upon that ignorance and to demonise one or more communities. (Cantle, 2008: 15)

Cantle (2008) considers the concept of segregation as monocultural with the aim being to focus on society and cultural diversity to allow a more multicultural outlook. The issue of the 'lack of contact' is also significant because if there is limited or no communication between different communities you have greater monoculturalism. Cantle Report (HO: 2001) described segregation as 'parallel lives' after the civil disturbances in Britain in 2001.[1] Cantle also conceptualizes segregation in two ways:

> it is possible to distinguish this 'exclusive' pattern of segregation from a more open 'critical mass' model, in which a given community is clustered in a particular area, but do not occupy it exclusively. Their concentration is sufficient to support a range of distinct cultural facilities and a support network that helps to preserve cultural identity whilst the presence of other groups within the same area means that contact and interaction can still be facilitated through shared local activities and by mixed intake schools and integrated employment and entrepreneurial arrangements. In these circumstances, they 'layers of separation' will not be cumulative and interaction will be able to take place at some level. (Cantle, 2008: 16)

Different degrees of segregation which can be total within an 'exclusive' pattern or partial within a 'critical mass' model, but whatever degree of segregation there is, social and cultural exclusion remains. Phillips (2005) was asking for greater communication between communities post 7/7, concerning not only issues relating to the terrorist attacks on London, but a focus on current issues that actually faced communities in Britain in 2005 for example, under achievement in education, poverty and racism. Coelho suggests that segregation,

> entails the legally enforced separation of different cultural and racial groups. Policies of segregation are designed to limit the participation of minorities in decision-making – even when the minorities actually constitute a numerical majority – and serve to ensure the continuing economic and political dominance of some groups and the subordination of others. (Coelho, 1998: 19)

Coelho (1998) uses examples from Apartheid South Africa and the United States prior to desegregation in the 1950s. The author suggests separate faith schools can be regarded as segregated schools and also urban and suburban areas can be culturally, economically and geographically segregated which is reflected in school demographics. Tomlinson states:

> in Britain there has never been official school segregation of children from different racial or ethnic groups, but de facto segregation has been steadily

> increasing, based on the reality that segregated housing patterns plus neighbourhood school policies lead inexorably to 'high immigrant' or 'black-minority' schools . . . However, it would seem that up to 1980 at least, most ethnic minority parents and their children are still, by and large, seeking pluralistic incorporation into the majority society via the English state education system, desiring the same kind of education and opportunities offered to white children. (Tomlinson, 1983: 15)

Tomlinson (1983) shows that segregation is nothing new and her research was published over twenty years before Phillips (2005) so this gives the reader an idea of how entrenched these ideas actually are in England. As shown in the previous chapter, parents were still seeing education in the pre-Swann era (DES, 1985) as an opportunity to climb a meritocratic ladder out of poverty by the power of education. Mulvaney (in Straker-Welds, 1984) produces evidence in England of segregation within schools and the social and cultural consequences this can have on children from Muslim, Sikh and Hindu communities. Racism was highlighted and measures to counter racism were recommended in the MacDonald Report into the murder of a 13-year-old Bangladeshi boy in a school playground in Manchester. Measures had to go further than what the MacDonald Report (Macdonald et al., 1989: 402) labelled as 'symbolic' or 'moral' anti-racism. It is disturbing that the Macdonald Report was published ten years before the MacPherson Report (1999) which was examined in the previous chapter. Both reports start with racially motivated incidents that led to the death of two individuals. The issue of race and racism remains and can be seen as a cause of social segregation (Rmaji, 2009).

Gilroy (1992: 313–14) underlines the importance of the social construction of race and the production of urban meanings for different cultures and communities. He argues: 'The idea of the city as a jungle where bestial, predatory values prevail preceded the large-scale settlement of Britain by blacks in the post-war-period'. The city can be described in different ways (Pratt-Adams et al., 2010) but the point here is that racism was not exclusively new nor was racial prejudice, described by Singh (in Lynch et al., 1992: 211) as, '. . . a social disease of epidemic proportions [and] . . . there has not yet been any unified, national effort in Britain to counteract its negative, all-pervading, damaging effects'. Overcoming racial prejudice by educating people about cultural differences seems an easy solution to a complex problem but something had and has to be continually done to overcome stereotypical thinking relating to minority communities. Singh continues by suggesting that prejudice is an affront to human rights and implies that a human rights education can address stereotypic views and racial prejudice which can begin to address racism and social segregation. However, social and cultural issues remain and have consequences for children's education. Gallagher (2004) highlights that residential segregation leads to school segregation which concerns children's performance and (under)achievement (Archer and Francis, 2007). Achievement and success within education is a key component for children and communities if they want to climb the meritocratic ladder.

Social interaction is raised as a key factor when reducing segregation and is highlighted by Tatum with the majority, white community in the United States having little or no contact with minority communities:

> 70 percent of white youth do not have such experiences with great frequency, the increase in interaction reported in this study can be seen as a positive result of improving race relations in the United States of America. What will the answers be in 2010? Or in 2020? (Tatum, 2007: 13–14)

Tatum's (2007) comment is useful because we are now about to examine what Phillips had to say about Britain 'Sleepwalking to Segregation', using the United States as an example of where, in his opinion, this had occurred. This section has shown how issues of racism and racial prejudice combined with stereotypical thinking and labelling leads to social segregation.

Reflective Exercise

- How are issues of segregation, racism, racial prejudice and stereotypical thinking all culturally and socially interlinked?

Was Britain 'sleepwalking to segregation'?

Having looked at the debates surrounding terror and social segregation, we now examine both the speech made by Phillips (2005) and respondent reactions who were interviewed for this book concerning the questions and issues that Phillips raised. The speech is important not only because of its context that is, a reaction to the immediate debates concerning 7/7, but also because it both highlighted and contributed to a general movement in policy-making in England away from multicultural towards integrationist conceptual ideas. Phillips (2005: 1–2) began his speech acknowledging the contribution the Centre for Racial Equality (CRE) had made in 'holding communities together' with a particular upsurge in anti-Asian activity in the post 7/7 period (Gereluk and Race, 2007). The aim, Phillips believed, was to work towards 'developing common bonds of identity' which initially implies that segregation needed to be at the least addressed within policy debates in Britain. However, Phillips does at this early stage of his speech mention a 'political goal' which draws on the governmental policy of community cohesion arising from the Cantle Report (HO, 2001). Phillips (2005) focuses on the issues raised in that report, relating to 'integration and accountability', themes of the *Every Child Matters* (HO, 2003) recommendations, which had not only educational, but social and cultural consequences for all communities and children in schools. Phillips is drawing on existing policy debates in England which have been shaped by the concept of integration (DfES, 2004). He draws on the United States as his example of a segregated society and uses the Hurricane Katrina flooding in New Orleans in 2005 to underline an educational truth where

> most black academics are teaching at all-black colleges or in urban institu-
> tions disproportionately packed with ethnic minority students. This is a
> segregated society, in which the one truth that is self-evident is that people
> cannot and never will be equal. This is why, for all of us who care about
> racial equality and integration, America is not our dream, but our nightmare.
> (Phillips, 2005: 5)

The fear for Phillips is that British society is becoming more divided along both racial and religious lines. The result for Philips (ibid.) is ' . . . a New Orleans-style Britain of passively co-existing ethnic and religious communities, eyeing each other uneasily over the fences of our differences'. And here is where Phillips believes we are sleepwalking our way to segregation. As he argues: 'We are becoming strangers to each other, and we are leaving communities to be marooned outside the mainstream' (ibid.).

When analysing the data collected for this book in relation to Philips 'sleepwalking to segregation' notion, it is significant to note in the exchange below that the idea of people becoming strangers to each other, raised by Phillips is mentioned and developed by the following interviewee who is a university lecturer:

- *University Lecturer – I think 'Sleepwalking to Segregation' is perhaps the negative, the worst case scenario in a way. The most negative spin on diversity, because it looks at the minimum of communities, particular social groupings, having minimum interaction, a minimum kind of engagement other than the fact they are functioning as part of society: working; paying taxes . . .*
- *Interviewer – Do you think it is a different reading of the notion of social cohesion? That segregation or segregated communities are cohesive but they are isolated. They are exclusive rather than inclusive. Do you think there are any elements of truth in that argument?*
- *University Lecturer – I think where it becomes segregated, segregation is when the cultural differences are very well, at the forefront of people's minds on both sides whereas on the one hand, it is the community that is segregated in terms of being in a particular part of the town and making up a population of a particular area. . . . [i.e.] . . . the discourse of strangers . . . We spend a lot of our time now communicating continuously on a virtual level. We are continually searching for meanings, social relations with people and making full use of technologies in that way. But there is an irony that at the same time this happens within a politics of fear and the politics of surveillance makes us feel more disengaged from our immediate, social, physical surroundings than perhaps it did before. [Anthony] Giddens talks about a disembeddedness and I think that is something that is very much felt especially by young people in cities like London. The discourse of strangers is the idea you can be spend all your time on the internet, e-mailing or texting people and you spend a huge amount of your time walking around surrounded by strangers, people who you have absolutely no kind of engagement with people who you sit on the bus with, people who you buy food from.*

The 'discourse of strangers' is a contemporary if uncomfortable idea. The university lecturer stated that he had drawn on Giddens (1998: 78–86) notion of civil society and community renewal within a research project but turned those ideas on their head. This gives us not only a perspective which is very different to community cohesion (HO: 2001) but an impression of society in the opening two decades of the twenty-first century. Globalization and technology, summarized by social networking virtual environments for example, Facebook and Twitter, have caused us to become socially separated and segregated on a number of different levels. This comment highlights the complexity of segregation by suggesting it does not only operate at just social and cultural, but technological and global levels. The segregation at these levels relates to two factors. First, who has the technology and facilities to socially network within virtual environments? Secondly, is the interviewee right when he suggests that we might be communicating with people who we will never see or meet, but not know a thing about someone we might pass in the street every day? This leads us back into Phillips' speech with analysis of viewpoints about present and future ideas concerning segregated communities. Phillips believes:

> We could have a different future. But if we want that different future, we have to put policies and programmes in place to stop the drift towards disaster. If we don't, two things will happen:
>
> - First, when the hurricane hits – and it could be a recession rather than a natural disaster, for example – those communities are set up for destruction.
> - And second, even if there is no calamity, these marooned communities will steadily drift away from the rest of us, evolving their own lifestyles, playing by their own rules and increasingly regarding the codes of behaviour, loyalty and respect that the rest of use take for granted as outdated behaviour that no longer applies to them. We know what follows then: crime, no-go areas and chronic cultural conflict. (Phillips, 2005: 5)

The 'discourse of strangers' argument counters Cantle's (2008) idea of community cohesion. Phillips (2005: 5–6) suggests, 'Residential isolation is increasing for many minority groups in England, especially South East Asians. Some minorities are moving into middle-class, less ethnically concentrated areas, but what is left behind is hardening in its separateness'. Phillips creates and uses an 'index of dissimilarity' to measure how segregated a district is:

> The [index] tells us what percentage of any given group would have to move house to achieve an even spread across the district. Below 30% is regarded as low or random . . . 30–60% is moderate . . . and above 60% is high . . . Happily, we aren't yet in this range – mostly. But too many communities, especially those of Pakistani and Bangladeshi heritage in some cities, are up around the 60s and the 70s even in London. (Phillips, 2005: 6)

The 'discourse of strangers' notion can also be applied to spatial segregation and Phillips (2005: 7) describes this as people ' . . . inhabit[ing] separate social and cultural worlds'. Phillips is claiming that Britain is not only becoming more segregated but also more exclusive in terms of who people are choosing to be sociable with. He sums up by acknowledging the 'pretty bleak picture' he has painted, but provides a potential solution to the problems of segregation. The aim, Phillips (ibid.) claims is to ' . . . start by deciding what we want to achieve. In my view, there are two clear priorities for government and the nation. Now: protection of citizens, and reassurance on security. Soon, very soon: maximising integration, minimising extremism'.

Phillips ends the above quote with the term integration which reminds us of the political context of documents examined in the last chapter (HO, 2001; 2003) which provided the background and context for his speech. The next section deals with his views on integration and multiculturalism but it is worth reflecting again on the notion of segregation and Phillips (2005) interpretation. Phillips does not go into great depth in relation to segregation and certainly does not draw on Cantle's (2008) notion of 'exclusive' and 'critical mass' segregation. The 'discourse of strangers' idea seems to be a more contemporary example to use than Phillips' 'index of dissimilarity' which is focused on minority communities rather than an inclusive focus which acknowledges the diversity within a whole population. The 'discourse of strangers' notion seems a more appropriate term to use when considering the possibility of Britain 'sleepwalking to segregation'.

Reflective Exercise

- Does 'the discourse of strangers' apply to societies in the present?
- Is the idea of 'community cohesion' still applicable today?

Trevor Phillips and the politics of integration

As has already been underlined, Phillips (2005), as chair of the CRE was reacting to a governmental integrationist policy that had been visible in both official reports (HO: 2001) and social policy (HO: 2003). Phillips' (2005: 7) comment on '. . . maximising integration, minimising extremism . . .' underlines the conceptual focus on integration which relates to state involvement and policy intervention. Terror and extremism have been examined in an earlier section of this chapter but we now examine Phillips' (2005) views on the concept of integration and its implications for multiculturalism. Integration was analysed in the previous chapter as a concept that came before multiculturalism in education and social policy debates. Phillips suggested that

> there has to be a balance struck between an 'anything goes' multiculturalism on the one hand, which leads to deeper division and inequality; and on the other, an intolerant, repressive uniformity. We need a kind of integration that binds us together without stifling us. We need to be a nation of many colours that combines to create a single rainbow. (Phillips, 2005: 3)

Phillips interpretation of multiculturalism suggests that an 'anything goes' concept needs to be replaced with something more substantial. Phillips is looking for an interpretation of integration that binds rather than stifles, implying the rainbow nation image flag which was an attempt to symbolize the cultural diversity of South Africa. However, Phillips warns of the danger of assimilationist possibilities:

> I believe we are in danger of throwing out the integrationist baby along with the assimilationist bathwater. In recent years, we've focused far too much on the 'multi' and not enough on the common culture. We've emphasized what divides us over what unites us. We have allowed tolerance of diversity to harden into the effective isolation of communities, in which some people think special separate values ought to apply. (ibid.)

It is significant that Phillips' uses the term 'assimilationist' which in the previous chapter highlighted a one-way social relationship. He then goes on to criticize multiculturalism which he believes should be replaced, in his own words, by a common culture focus. This, it is suggested, can be achieved within an integrationist conceptual framework which looks for majority cultural values that is, the common culture, being accepted by minority communities. Phillips perceives the aftermath of the London terrorist attacks of the 7th and 21st of July 2005 provided opportunities to bring people together within a British common culture. This perception, even within a notion of increased community cohesion (HO, 2001; Cantle, 2008) becomes problematic if communities – both majority and minority – resist forms of social and cultural integration. However, Phillips argues that

> integration has to be a two-way street in which the settled communities accept that new people will bring change with them. Newcomers realise that

they too will have to change if we are to move closer to an integrated society. (Phillips, 2005: 4)

Phillips moreover suggests what he believes an integrated society should look like with three essential features:

- Equality, everyone is treated equally . . .
- Participation: all groups in society should expect to share in how we make decisions . . .
- Interaction: no-one should be trapped within their community, and in the truly integrated society, who people work with, or the friendships they make, should not be constrained by race or ethnicity. (ibid.)

Equality, participation and interaction are therefore the characteristics of Phillips' integrated Britain. This implies an extension of the idea of community cohesion that Cantle (HO, 2001) raised, but notions of racism and racial prejudice which create social division and segregation are not mentioned here. Phillips touches upon greater anti-discrimination as one possibility of producing more community cohesion and uses the educational system of the United States that addressed school segregation in the 1950s to show how integration had failed to bring majority and minority children together in schools. Integrationist policy, Phillips (2005: 4) believes the need for more than a reliance on law. Integration has to be prepared for. The state and therefore the education system need to be prepared for 'Newcomers'. As Phillips argues,

We know that the next generation's migrants won't look like the last. They are likely to be more European, more diverse in their origins, not English speaking. Whatever their faith – Somali Muslims, Polish Catholics, African Evangelicals – they will, unlike most of us, probably take that faith very seriously and live by what they profess. (Phillips, 2005: 5)

So, faith schools and all schools, in Phillips' (2005) view, have to be continually prepared for the influx of new migrants from all over the world. This school preparation for new migrants is clearly along integrationist rather than multicultural lines. However, it has to be acknowledged that Phillips (2005) is at least trying to offer possible solutions to segregation with integrationist ideas. Whether a two-way relationship is conditional or otherwise is immaterial when the aim is to get people interacting and moving away from society 'sleepwalking into segregation' or the 'discourse of strangers' notions. As he suggests, people will not interact within societies if there are low levels of community participation and high levels of social inequality. A potential solution is Cantle's (HO: 2001) notion of community cohesion which Phillips (2005) fails to mention.

Phillips suggests that the cultural picture may be improving:

> But we do start with a great advantage, modern Britain is ready for the challenge of integration. [Centre for Racial Equality] CRE research shows that for the first time in sixty years we are growing more relaxed about our ethnic differences. (Phillips, 2005:7)

Phillips fails to elaborate on how relaxed British society is about ethnic difference. Despite this omission, the intention is clear in Phillips' words: '. . . we need to be sure that newcomers will fit in'. And the conditions for 'newcomers' need to be specific and include the following:

> first, a job or qualifications, and demonstrable skills including English; second, good health; and third, some evidence of loyalty to Britain. In short, we are looking for migrants who have the ability to participate in our national life, and the willingness to interact with the rest of us. (Phillips, 2005: 8)

So, alongside the 'essentials' of 'equality, interaction and participation', Phillips, it seems, is looking for migrants to be: well off; qualified; healthy; English speaking; who will ultimately show loyalty to Britain. This is a very exclusive opinion and is more assimilationist than integrationist which Phillips ironically attempts to avoid earlier in his speech. The 'essentials' which Phillips describes are conditional qualities that 'newcomers' need to show when interacting and participating socially. The aim of multiculturalism is to celebrate difference (Parekh, 2008) rather than promoting a conditional integrationist, almost assimilationist list of conditions for incoming migrants.

Interpretations of Phillips' arguments

This section continues to highlight how respondents felt about Phillips (2005) speech and aims to give a balanced account of viewpoints when considering not only multiculturalism and education issues but whether the concept of multiculturalism has a contemporary relevance and application (Eade et al.,

2008). Phillips himself implies a necessary focus on the 'essentials' of 'equality, interaction and participation'. However, a combination of: two university teacher trainer's; three university lecturer's; and, one postgraduate student experiences below from the interviews for this book, examine viewpoints on whether multiculturalism is dead:

- *University Teacher Trainer (1) – I think he [Phillips] was right on several accounts [He] . . . probably exaggerates that multiculturalism policies are defunct. Multiculturalism as a philosophy is not defunct, but is maybe redundant, needs to be revived, needs to be invigorated, needs to be connected to real social movements and change. I think it was important . . . it meant the debate was brought into the public sphere and that was very important.*
- *University Lecturer (1) – He [Phillips] might be correct but I think the big issue is people have different definitions of what multiculturalism is. So, I think he may be referring to the kind of people who think, 'Oh yes, everyone has the right to live their ways'. It's fine that people are living parallel lives and that kind of thing. You are living together but there is an over-arching theme or thing bringing people together. So, I think it is difficult to answer that question in that sense because it depends on what one means by multiculturalism.*
- *University Teacher Trainer (2) – I think it depends on how you define multiculturalism. I think from my own experience I've seen an awful lot of what has come under the label multiculturalism which effectively to me was tokenism. And I think that type of multiculturalism is dead because it's probably done more damage than good. And therefore it needs something different and redefining.*
- *University Lecturer (2) – I think people are finding the notion of multiculturalism more problematic now because it implies a certain kind of level of convergence, some sort of cultural convergence which I suppose with the kind of media stories and the way politics is in this country, it's becoming more and more of a kind of, it's reverting back to, a utopian idea rather than a reality. I know from my own knowledge of the subject that the buzz word of multiculturalism has very much been replaced by the buzz word of diversity. Diversity, I think, is perhaps a more kind of half way house or realistic notion and it is something very much spoken about in contemporary politics.*

- *Postgraduate Student – He [Phillips] was incorrect because there are within the UK a variety of different communities, up and down the length of the land . . . communities that have worked together, continued to work together. Of course there are fractions but everywhere you look, particularly at cultural events . . . in some occasions political events, in the way in which communities come together around particular political issues and cultural issues, I think there are clear examples of multiculturalism not being dead as a phenomenon.*
- *University Lecturer (3) – Well, no. I don't see how you can simply say it's dead or it isn't. I think the interesting thing about all these debates is it has caused a lot of questioning and introspection and rightly so, about what multiculturalism is and what it means and whether of course it is effective. I think it is silly to say it is dead. How could it be dead? It's not a living being (laughs). At the same time, I think obviously it is right to say there is a lot of critique and thought going into the notion of multiculturalism.*

University lecturer (1) and university teacher trainer (1) think Phillips is 'right' or 'maybe correct' in arguing that multiculturalism is dead. There were other respondents in both questionnaires and interviews that agreed in principal with the idea that multiculturalism was not relevant. In this sense, critical feelings about multiculturalism at the very least highlights, in some peoples eyes, its contemporary irrelevance. University teacher trainer (1) and university teacher trainer (2) revert to what the actual definition or definitions of multiculturalism are. Multiculturalism can mean different things to different people (Levy, 2000; Parekh, 2008; Eade et al., 2008). This underlines the complexity of any conceptual debate, be it multiculturalism or integration for example. University lecturer (2) highlights the problematic nature of the concept of multiculturalism and adds a fourth 'essential' to Phillips' integrationist framework, the idea of diversity. This idea is inclusive in the sense that by including all migrants, regardless of qualification and ability, all cultures are theoretically represented which is multicultural in orientation. The postgraduate student and university lecturer (3) disagree with Phillips and criticize the use of the word 'dead', one as a phenomenon and the other within an ongoing multicultural debate. Multiculturalism, for university lecturers (2) and (3), as well as the postgraduate student, is very much alive although the concept needs to be reviewed and debated within ongoing social discourses.

Phillips argues that segregation has to be addressed through education and minimized through social and cultural change. He states that, we find that young people are daily separated in the place where they spend the greatest part of their time: schools and universities. . . . we cannot simply stand by and see the next generation schooled to become strangers. (Phillips, 2005: 9)

This not only concerns the 'discourse of strangers' image which was developed earlier in this chapter but highlights that segregation can exclude children within schools and the education system (Archer and Francis, 2007). Education needs to focus on issues of achievement for young people from all communities by bringing them socially and culturally together with more culturally diverse curricula (Banks, 2009) rather than excluding them within education policy designed within integrationist conceptual frameworks.

We move on to show a university lecturer's response in interview to the issues surrounding the second question in the chapter title relating to whether Britain was 'sleepwalking to segregation'.

> University Lecturer – If you look at certain areas of London [e.g.] Wembley, Southall . . . these are areas that have become segregated, 99%, if not more in areas of Leicester, Birmingham, Bradford, Oldham and Burnley there is segregation. Whether we are sleepwalking into it is something that I don't think is the case. People are aware of this, it is not something that has happened without people actively involved in the process . . . I think everyone is aware and everyone is actively involved in the process. So, to call it sleepwalking is wrong. Segregation itself is happening, has happened and continues to happen but it is not a passive process.

The interviewee claims that segregation is occurring but is an active and conscious process rather than an unconscious one. This suggests that people are consciously segregating themselves from other communities. If this is the case, people are hardly 'sleepwalking' as they are socially and culturally moving into communities which provide them with the most cohesion. This provides a new angle to Cantle's (2008) notion of community cohesion and is also critical of the term which Phillips (2005) is using.

Summary

What this chapter has attempted to show is that Phillips' (2005) speech was not created in a political or social vacuum. His views were a response not only to 7/7 but a governmental agenda which had been influenced by a more integrationist policy framework (HO, 2001; 2003; DfES, 2004). His speech was a political response to multiculturalism and segregation and respondent evidence in this chapter both agreed and disagreed with his views on whether multiculturalism is dead or whether Britain was 'sleepwalking into segregation'. Phillips challenged multicultural assumptions by claiming that integrationist ideas were better in a contemporary context and by claiming multiculturalism was dead. He was contributing to a debate, highlighted earlier in this chapter, by Sen (2006) which was taking place in other countries for example, France and the United States. Conceptual debates are amongst many things, social and situational (Mason, 1995) so Phillips, as the then Chair of the CRE in 2005, was responding to what was going on in England at that time. Although his comments on multiculturalism as a concept and a phenomenon can be questioned having looked at the evidence in previous chapters of this book, it can be argued he was correct to highlight continuing social and cultural segregation. As Finney and Simpson suggest in relation to Phillips' ideas on segregation:

> The argument is generally that 'the pace of change' in local neighbourhoods arising from ideas and behaviour new to Britain has led to retreat by religious and ethnic groups into 'their own communities' such that people of different communities are living separate and parallel lives. (Finney and Simpson, 2009: 6)

On the one hand, Philips (2005) when highlighting social separation and segregation was reacting to extreme events and government policy, although he fails to mentions the Cantle Report (HO: 2001) and the notion of community cohesion (Cantle, 2008). On the other hand, the terms 'sleepwalking' and 'dead' were not the most appropriate ones he could have used in the circumstances.

Phillips' (2005: 3) use of the term 'two-way street' also has uncomfortable comparisons with the conditional 'two-way' relationships which were highlighted when examining the concept of integration in the previous chapter. The problematic nature of both integration and multiculturalism in the twenty-first century has led to a fascinating ongoing debate (e.g. Goodhart, 2006; Pathak, 2007; Eade et al., 2008; Finney and Simpson, 2009). Another issue that has been touched upon several times in the first half of this book, and particularly by Phillips (2005) is the role of education in faith schools. The next chapter deals with issues concerning faith schools and the idea of multi-faith schools which allows us to increase our understandings of the complexity and contemporary nature of multiculturalism and education.

Useful websites

Equality and Human Rights Commission
  www.equalityhumanrights.com/
London Attacks
  http://news.bbc.co.uk/1/hi/in_depth/uk/2005/london_explosions/default.stm
Remember Segregation
  http://remembersegregation.org/

Note

1. The civil disturbances in the North of England in 2001 occurred before the attacks on the Twin Towers in New York City in September 2001.

4 Faith Schools and Multiculturalism

Chapter Outline

Introduction

Faith schools are being examined as a contemporary issue in education because in England, debates in the last decade have become more political as the evidence in this chapter will highlight. Faith schools, as Gordon and Lawton (2003: 32) underline, is a '. . . term used to embrace schools under the auspices of different denominations'. 'Faith' is a term which can be described as a system of religious belief. In England, the major but not exclusive providers of faith schooling are the Church of England and Roman Catholic Churches. Faith schooling has a continuing part to play in today's society and to increase understanding of the complexity of that role; we have to acknowledge some of the key events and moments in the history of faith schools in England. However, this can only be a short historical section which examines, among other things, the relationship between state and the churches regarding the funding of education. This is followed by an examination of issues surrounding the faith and multi-faith school debate – multi-faith schooling meaning curricula that includes and involves children in different religious beliefs – which has implications for multiculturalism and education. Education policy will also be analysed to see whether a more inclusive, multi-faith focus is also possible (DfEE, 2001; DfES, 2002; DCSF, 2007).

A short history concerning English faith schools

Faith schools have a history in England that goes back hundreds of years, acknowledged by Aldrich below, before the first state grant was granted to education in 1833:

> The major divisions which emerged in the Christian church in the west in the sixteenth century have lasted until this day. Judaism apart, however, other religions than Christianity have had little place in English society, until the advent of large scale Commonwealth immigration, particularly from the Indian sub-continent in the second half of the twentieth century. Thus educational ideas have been constructed within a Christian context. (Aldrich, 1982: 23)

The Christian church's existence and the funding of education had been crucial to the establishment of universal education at elementary (primary) and then secondary levels. The issues of permanence and financing are vital when considering faith schools in any country. That religious influence and expenditure into education would mean that it would be very difficult to remove faith schools as education systems would face difficulties due to the loss of the financial resources that different denominations provide. The French system of education provides an interesting comparison with the English education system in relation to faith schooling. Green (1991: 130–70) provides a excellent account concerning how a French system of secular education evolved from Napoleonic reforms that centralized education and promoted French nationalism and identity in the nineteenth century. Saunders (in Levey and Modood, 2009: 70–81) shows how the law of separation of church from state did not take place in France until 1905. This was not to be the case in England. As McKinney (in McKinney, 2008: 2) highlights, both the Catholic and Church of England realized the dangers of increasing secularism. They refused to fully incorporate their schools into the growing state maintained sector without recognition that their faiths and systems of belief would remain in schools. Faith schools had to be aware of secularist interests and adapt: 'Objection to Canterbury and Rome on the rates was not a new development' (Morris, 2003: 290). Smith (2009) provides a fascinating account of how different denominational faiths in England towards the end of the nineteenth century adapted, joined and participated within the new system of School Boards introduced in 1870, to run the system of compulsory education for young children.

The 1944 Education Act provided an option for faith schooling: Voluntary Controlled or Voluntary status. McKinney explains the distinction:

> Voluntary Controlled schooling guaranteed local authority funding and management, but also some guarantees concerning denominational religious instruction. Voluntary Aided schooling entailed local authority funding for all running costs, but churches remained as 'custodial trustees' and were responsible for 50% of capital building costs. Later the state contribution would rise to 75% (1959), 80% (1967) and 85% (1975). (McKinney in McKinney, 2008: 3)

The 1944 Education Act also made religious instruction and daily acts of worship statutory obligations for schools but parents had the legal right to withdraw their child from these obligations, if it did not interfere with pupils' attendance (Dent, 1962: 24–28). The financial issue of resourcing was now connected with the practical issue of religious instruction in faith schools. During the second half of the twentieth century, other faiths were also becoming more influential within the faith school debate as Jackson highlights:

> The fact that some Jewish voluntary aided schools were established in 1944 has lent weight to the argument that other non-Christian religious bodies should apply for certain independent schools to be granted Voluntary Aided status. There was an attempt to establish a Hindu Voluntary Aided school in the 1970s. The proposed co-educational comprehensive school (the Vivekanada Hindu High School) was to be situated in London, catering for around a thousand children from Hindu families . . . Several Muslim independent schools attempted to obtain Voluntary Aided status during the 1980s and 1990s. (Jackson, 2001: 3)

The fact that both Hindu and Muslim attempts should succeed or fail in the 1980s and 1990s is not the main issue here, the fact that non-Christian faiths were attempting to open schools to accommodate their religions is the significant point. The issue was becoming more political because the state was having to decide on whether different faiths could open schools in England.

The Labour Government of the 1990s was prepared to allow independent schools with non-Christian traditions to become Voluntary Aided. The evidence suggests that this movement had been gathering momentum for decades (Jackson, 2001). As Parker-Jenkins et al. underline:

> Between 1986 and 2002 there were 16 Education Acts and the partnership between Church and state continued to develop through various reforms and changes but the School Standards and Framework Act (1998) is noteworthy because it contains a number of provisions which bring faith-based school communities substantially into the decision-making process. The Act created four categories of schools within the state system in England and Wales:
>
> - Community Schools (formerly County schools
> - Foundation Schools (formerly Grant Maintained schools);
> - Voluntary Aided Schools; and,
> - Voluntary Controlled Schools. (Parker-Jenkins et al., 2005: 17)

It is important to highlight how the state was encouraging collective agreement at all levels between state and church. It is also significant to consider which faiths would benefit most from this relationship. The Education White Paper (DfEE, 2001) called for faith school expansion in England. As the DCSF (2007: 2) explained, between 1997 and 2007: '. . . Muslim, Sikh, Seventh Day Adventist and Greek Orthodox schools have also joined the maintained sector and other Christian denominations have entered into joint denominational partnerships'. However, the development of academy schools with a religious character have been created by Christian churches and Christian collaborations, not the faiths mentioned in the above quote (DCSF, 2007; Walford, 2008). As Jackson highlights, this monopoly of faith school development caused problems:

> The position that religious education in state-funded Community schools should be taught from a Christian perspective in order to inculcate Christian belief was rejected, as were the views that it is justifiable in such schools to teach Christianity as true in order to foster a particular brand of personal and social morality or for historical and cultural reasons. The standpoint that religious education should be confined to the study of Christianity was also held to be unsustainable in the light of social plurality . . . and the forces of globalization. (Jackson, 2004: 161)

The near monopoly of faith school expansion in England was problematic because it was based on Christianity. The failure to acknowledge increased cultural diversity, multiculturalism and the need for non-Christian denominations to practice their religions are contemporary political issues. This 'unsustainable' position that Jackson mentions above is influenced by the context which this section has highlighted. The history of faith schools involves churches investing money in their schools. Faith schools have had to contend and compete with state influence since 1833 in England (Stephens, 1998). This financial commitment is ongoing in England, but is different in France due to the secularization of French education which was achieved in 1905. Issues of faith schooling have always been political but the changing cultural diversity and multiculturalism of countries has encouraged different faiths to open their own schools. As Parker-Jenkins et al. (2005: 37) show, contemporary outlooks on faith schools have introduced new factors into the debate: 'The expansion of faith-based schools can be seen as part of a government strategy to extend provision of a category of schools which it sees as being successful in terms of parental support and academic attainment'. Parents have seen the opportunities for children of relatively successful faith schools and have been prepared to physically move their families into the catchment areas of these schools (Ball, 2003). The issue here concerns the numbers of faith schools rather than schools and their relative success in education terms and funding, be it from a faith, the state or both. In the next sections we will see how the state in England has attempted to address the issue of expanding faith schooling while at the same time attempting to recognize more denominations within society, thereby theoretically recognizing changing cultural diversity and increased multiculturalism.

Reflective Exercise

- What are the current advantages and disadvantages of faith schooling?

State support for faith schools

Two education policy documents are being examined to gain a greater understanding into the promotion of faith schools (*Schools – Building on Success –* DfEE, 2001; *Schools Achieving Success –* DfES, 2002). It is worth remembering that the inner city riots in the north-west of England took place in 2001, as well as the attacks on the Twin Towers in New York in the same year. These contextual events would have shaped policy discussion, not only those concerning state support for faith schools (Bleich, 2009). However, Walford (2008) highlights that Tony Blair, as Prime Minister supported the idea of expanding faith schools before 2001 and the two education policy documents were significant in that desire. Both education documents have the word *success* in their titles and they also allow for the potential expansion of faith schools. The first policy document was a Green Paper that is, a consultation document, which contained the following passage:

> Schools supported by the churches and other major faith groups are, of course, valued by members of those groups. They also have a good record of delivering a high-quality of education to their pupils and many parents welcome the clear ethos of these schools. We therefore wish to welcome more schools provided by the churches and other major faith groups and by other voluntary and community groups, where there is clear local demand from parents and the community. We are pleased, for example, to see that Lord Dearing's report to the Archbishops' Council that recommends the Church of England increase the number of secondary schools that it supports, particularly in areas where there are few or no Anglican schools. We know other faith communities are also interested in extending their contribution to education. We intend to change the capital funding arrangements to make them more favourable to enable this to occur. (DfEE, 2001)

The 'high quality of education' delivered by faith schools is an issue here because high achieving schools within an education market had become attractive to parents who could get their children into these schools. The issue raised by Ball (2003) is significant in that schools are not open to all within the education market and therefore this opportunity would only be available to parents having the cultural capital when choosing a school for their children. The Church of England can also strategically expand by increasing their financial levels of support for secondary schools. Other faith communities are mentioned but not defined and capital funding arrangements, it is implied, would become 'more favourable' for other communities. Yet again, the term 'more favourable' is very vague with no specific mentioning of faith communities. The second education policy document (DfES, 2002) develops the idea of community partnership by claiming that the government would support faith schools:

> Faith schools have a significant history as part of the state education system, and play an important role in its diversity. Over the last four years, we have

> increased the range and faith schools in the maintained sector, including the
> first Muslim, Sikh and Greek Orthodox schools. There are also many indepen-
> dent faith schools and we know that some faith groups are interested in
> extending their contribution to state education. We wish to welcome faith
> schools, with their distinctive ethos and character into the maintained sector
> where there is clear local agreement . . . Decisions to establish faith schools
> should take account to the interests of all sections of the community . . . We
> want faith schools that come into the maintained sector to add to the inclu-
> siveness and diversity of the school system and to be ready to work with
> non-denominational schools and those of other faiths. (DfES, 2002: 45)

The introduction of state maintained schools from the Muslim, Sikh and Greek Orthodox communities is a political move in a new direction that is, a potential movement which would allow other faith groupings to open new faith schools. The incentive for independent faith schools, 'with local agreement', is also being encouraged and welcomed by the state. It is being recommended by the DfES (2002), as it was in the Cantle Report (HO, 2001), that faith schools have a bigger role to play within community partnership and cohesion. That idea was endorsed by the Runnymede Report on *The Future of Multi-Ethnic Britain*, chaired by Bhikhu Parekh, which recommended the implementation of several points in relation to religion and belief:

- We recommend that in all faith communities there be closer connections between anti-racism and work to improve inter-faith relations.
- We recommend that legislation be introduced in Britain prohibiting
  direct and indirect discrimination on grounds of religion or belief . . .
  We recommend that a statement of general principles be drawn up
  on reasonable accommodation in relation to religious and cultural
  diversity in the workplace and in schools, and that case-study examples of good practice be provided.
- We recommend that a commission on the role of religion in the public life of a multi-faith society be set up to make recommendations on
  legal and constitutional matters. (Runnymede Trust, 2000: 233–43)

Improving inter-faith relations can be seen in both DfEE (2001) and DfES (2002) education policy documents. The drawing up of general principles of cultural diversity in the workplace and school is not mentioned in the education policy documents, that debate would have to wait until the Ajegbo Report (DfES, 2007) on citizenship and diversity which is examined in the next chapter. One of the urgent tasks that Parekh (2000: 265–66) suggests is: 'The need to recognize that Britain comprises a range of "majority" and "minority" communities which are internally diverse and which are changing'. Faith schools should thus have a role to play in striking a balance, recognizing not only diversity within communities, but diversity which continues to change. This is an appropriate statement as a year before the MacPherson Report (1999) was recommending that more cultural diversity be included within the national curriculum. As Pilkington explains:

> By visualising Britain as a community of communities and a community of citizens, the [Parekh] report expresses support for the three principles of cohesion, equality and difference . . . Some 'common values are necessary to hold [Britain] together and give it cohesion' . . . These are two forms: procedural and substantive. Procedural values are those such as tolerance, mutual respect and rationality, which provide 'the basic preconditions for democratic dialogue'. Substantive values are those enshrined in international human rights standards which 'underpin any defensible conception of the good life'. (Pilkington, 2003: 267)

Parekh (2000) and Cantle Report (HO: 2001) were looking for more community cohesion but in different ways; Parekh from a multicultural perspective, Cantle from an integrationist viewpoint. And both procedural and substantive values mentioned by Pilkington (2003) were covered in the DfEE (2001) and DfES (2002) education policy documents. Democratic dialogue was taking place with the possibility of an expansion of different faith schools combined with the need for an increasing culturally diverse focus. Faith schools could assist with producing more social and cultural cohesion in both the United Kingdom and the United States (Annette in Gardner et al., 2005). This has been developed in Department of Children, Schools and Families (DCSF) (2007) policy although this still seems to have a Christian focus and funding monopoly (Walford, 2008), as the evidence suggests below:

> Around one third of the total number of maintained schools in England are schools with a religious character (approximately 6,850 maintained schools with a religious character, out of a total of around 21,000 maintained schools). Of 47 Academies opened, 16 had a faith designation. There were three Church of England, one Roman Catholic, one Anglican/Roman Catholic and 11 non denominational Christian. Nearly 2 out of every 5 independent schools in England have a religious character (around 900 independent schools with a religious character out of a total of just over 2,300 independent schools). Over 700 of these independent schools represent various Christian denominations; the next largest numbers are 115 independent Muslim schools and 38 independent Jewish schools. (DCSF, 2007: 3)

Reflective Exercise

- Why are faith schools so attractive today to parents?
- What implications do the DCSF (2007:3) figures in the previous quote have for non-Christian schools in England?

Faith schools and cultural diversity

Parekh (2000) and Cantle Report (HO, 2001) highlighted the need for society to show what they described as greater community involvement, partnership and cohesion. Grace (2003: 161) argues that this public 'external enquiry' needs to be balanced alongside a faith schools 'own mission'. Grace (ibid.) describes this mission as '. . . love, peace, harmony, forgiveness and reconciliation' within wider community relations. The idea of a 'mission' underlined by Grace (2003) partly concerns faith schools, multiculturalism and community cohesion. Flint (2007: 264) suggests that community cohesion, '. . . remains tantalisingly out of reach in society [with] schools act[ing] as sites where existent conflicts and ambiguities are played out as well as generating divisions'. This highlights a contradiction within schools who attempt to provide social and cultural cohesion through in Grace's (2003) term, 'their mission', when they also have to deal with cultural difference and conflict (Ramsey, 2004).

There were a range of responses given for this book by both students at undergraduate and postgraduate levels, university teacher trainer and teacher trainee within the questionnaires and interviews to faith school experience and what had been taught in the classroom. The comment below – from a university teacher trainer – focuses on the question of curriculum and the complexity of delivering a culturally diverse syllabus within a faith school:

> *University Teacher Trainer – I think it depends on each individual school and I'm sure some schools are doing a really good job and some schools could do more. Even if they follow the same curriculum there are so many ways in which people can interpret it.*

The issue of interpretation of the curriculum does not only apply to students of different faiths and from different countries. It applies to teachers who have to cope with cultural diversity in the classroom. Dlamini and Martinovic (2007) explain the challenges teacher trainees in Canada face in relation to different languages spoken in the classroom. Santoro (2009) shows how pre-service teachers in Australia have simplistic understandings of students' cultures and their own constructed identities. The comment above from the university teacher trainer highlights that some schools are doing a good job in relation to cultural diversity and inter-faith curricula and experiences. The contemporary issue in education here revolves around the need to increase understandings of culturally diverse classrooms and all education environments within *all* schools.

Reflective Exercise

- How can all schools do more to make their curriculum more accessible to students from different cultural backgrounds?

The comment below from a university lecturer addresses the subject of whether faith schools should or could be more culturally diverse:

University Lecturer – Yes, otherwise we are talking about the worst form of segregation. When we talk about faith schools and if we are to promote multiculturalism, they have to acknowledge the fact that there is respect. A school can promote a particular faith but we also have to respect other peoples' faith, their ideological predilections, how they understand God [or many Gods] and how they are involved in these religious activities. So, yes we have to be very careful in relation to faith schools.

This comment relates to issues concerning segregation which were covered in the last chapter. The implication is that faith schools should be willing to engage with different faith based ideas. This in itself is a very multicultural idea for education that is, children not only being included and involved but also taught about different faiths and beliefs in subjects other than religion for example, citizenship. However, Rex (in Sikes and Rizvi, 1997:14) suggests there is '... [a] conservative lobby which argues that Religious Education should be "predominately Christian."' Moreover, this singular based idea of faith schooling is the major obstacle to multi-faith schooling. Santoro (2007) also acknowledges that if we are going to have multi-faith and culturally diverse schools, we are going to have to recruit and retain more teachers from culturally diverse backgrounds in all schools.

Reflective Exercise

• Can you provide examples from your educational experiences of multi-faith schooling?

The arguments for multi-faith and mono-faith schools

We now return to Trevor Phillips (2005) and what he had to say in his speech about faith schools and whether he believed multi-faith schooling is indeed possible. Phillips (2005: 6) argues: 'If faith schools are here to stay . . . what is to be taught in schools? Multi-faith schooling is culturally diverse but mono-faith schools intentionally segregate in a desire to put across a unique and individual set of religious values'. As has been already suggested, segregation is a complex issue (Ryan, 1999; Archer and Francis, 2007; Guibernau, 2007). Mckinney (2004) gives an example of how the Jewish community in Glasgow shaped their community identity though a Jewish primary school, but without a Jewish secondary school. The consequences of a secondary school not existing had short and medium term consequences for the Jewish community in Glasgow. This involved parents moving their children to an area which had a secondary school, leading to potentially greater segregation of the Jewish community to congregate in areas close to Jewish secondary school. The issue of increased segregation arises, in this case, out of the lack of educational choice caused by the state's reluctance to meet a faith and community demand that is, a Jewish secondary school, which is the issue here (Rex in Sikes and Rizvi, 1997).

In relation to general segregation, Phillips argues:

> Why does all this matter? First, for the obvious moral reason that no human being should have their destiny determined by the colour of their skin. And second, because segregation destroys talent. The evidence shows the quality of school in the United States is also colour coded: most black children are in rubbish schools, most whites in good ones. (Phillips, 2005: 7)

Phillips (ibid.) should have been more careful here when using a term like 'rubbish schools' as he provides no educational evidence to back up this claim. Education research from the United States (Massey and Fischer, 2006; Urrieta,

2006) and Europe (Van Houtte and Stevens, 2009) suggests that Phillips may have a point in relation to segregation and schooling. Faith schooling is more historical and religiously complex than using social and cultural segregation as a single reason for promoting mono-faith or multi-faith schooling. As Parker-Jenkins et al. highlight:

> From our research of Muslim schools in Britain and elsewhere during the last decade, we have found that in terms of full-time education, both state-funded and independent, there are both 'Muslim schools', and 'schools for Muslims', and it is important to distinguish between the two. In the former case, the intention is to develop an entire ethos consistent with religious values, rather than in the latter a school characterised by a shared religious identity but one which does not for much further in terms of developing curricula and ethos, often due to staffing and financial difficulties. (Parker-Jenkins et al., 2005: 40)

The distinction between state-funded and independent faith schools made by Parker-Jenkins et al. (ibid.) is an important one as historically, educational independence has offered the possibility of faith teaching a 'mission' (Grace, 2003) or 'ethos' which covers religious and cultural identity being taught in schools. Parker-Jenkins et al. (2005) also explain how Muslim immigration into The Netherlands has led to the opening of Dutch Muslim schools at both primary and secondary levels. These educational developments are by no means unique within Islamic education, and research continues into the ongoing debate concerning how Islamic values are taught within both 'Western', 'Middle Eastern' and global environments (Albrecht, 2007; Halstead, 2007; Khuram, 2007; Milligan, 2008; Ramadan, 2009).

Children's level of attainment measured by what qualifications they gained is examined from a number of community perspectives in England (Archer and Francis, 2007). Modood (2005: 96) suggests that minority communities, '. . . foster high expectations (even to the point of pressuring the children), give encouragement, maintain discipline (e.g. ensuring that homework is done), send children to and help with supplementary classes . . .'. Triandafyllidou et al. (2006: 3) also explain that, 'The relation between Muslims and the European societies in which they live has to be seen in terms of rising agendas of multiculturalism where Muslims have become central to these agendas as an exemplary "problem case"'. However, a focus on Muslim communities 'as the problem', exposes and contests the narrow definitions of racism and equality and the secular bias of the discourse and policy of multicultural education around the world: 'The issue is moving on from 'problem cases' and addressing the unique and complex issues that concern multicultural and multi-faith communities' (Open Society Institute, 2005). The need for increased understanding of relations *within and between* faith based communities is important in education, social and cultural contexts (Griffin, 2006; Eade et al., 2008). Castelli and Trevathon (2006) offer a Muslim perspective concerning the issues surrounding cultural diversity and the complexity all faith communities face:

> Young Muslims hear and participate in 'the prevailing patterns of reasoning and content of argument' of contemporary English society and are necessarily influenced by these. The values of materialism, consumerism and individualism are paraded before Muslim children, as they are before all children in Western society. The choice for the Muslim community, when raising their children in this context, is either to try and isolate their children from contemporary influences, and success in this is not assured, or to listen to their children's experiences, understand and respect these experiences and, through dialogue, to explore a Muslim spirituality that responds to them. The challenge for the sympathetic non-Muslim, including the teacher, is to listen to, and hear, the Muslim community's experience of this undertaking, recognising that they are not alone in seeking a spirituality that will match the task.
> (Castelli and Trevathon, in Johnson, 2006: 11)

The issue of listening to children, young adults and communities is crucial when increasing understanding of all faith based and multicultural communities, which will potentially increase the possibilities for greater community cohesion (HO: 2001; Cantle, 2008). There are other issues which concern different nation states and faith communities. Parker-Jenkins et al. raise the contradiction which faces all faith schools when they explain:

> the notion of state funding for any faith-based school could be seen as undermining the collective good of society as a whole. Yet to deny the children of religious parents the right of access to faith-based education also implies that moral values and ethical codes can be universally determined and applied to all, regardless of community desires. (Parker-Jenkins et al., 2005: 199–200)

And that's the contradiction that a debate concerning multiculturalism, faith schooling and community cohesion has to address (Flint, 2007). The issues concern nation states and faith schools finding a balance between expenditure issues with 'ethical codes' and the consideration of diverse community interests. As Parker-Jenkins et al. continue:

> Clearly the introduction of new faith-based schools in receipt of state funding presents an opportunity to those who believe that there should be not only diversity in provision, but also a much closer formal and informal relationship between different categories in schools. Added to this is a desire to see the development of closer working relationships between teachers and pupils across a range of diverse educational institutions. Although the path ahead may be strewn with obstacles, many of them are our own making. There has never been a better time to review and renew out commitment to an education for all. (Parker-Jenkins et al., 2005: 203–04)

And '. . . an education for all' has to accommodate both mono-faith and multi-faith schooling. Education research has to continue to analyse the arguments for both mono-faith and multi-faith schooling because if we are going to develop more closer, informal relationships between different faiths in schools, as Parker-Jenkins et al. (ibid.) recommend, these are going to be educationally focused on difference across subject areas that is, not only religious education or studies, which also relate to faith and culture.

The possibility of a more inclusive focus in faith schools

The final section of this chapter analyses the DCSF (2007) education policy document which calls for an increase in faith schools and an examination of the role of schools with a religious character in England. It also examines interviewee reaction to this possibility. That possibility is highlighted in the education policy recommendations below:

- Promote community cohesion. In this context, faith schools and their faith communities welcome the duty imposed on the governing bodies of all maintained schools in the Education and Inspections Act (DfES, 2006) to promote community cohesion . . .
- Work in a spirit of partnership with the local authority . . . as commissioners of education . . .
- Endeavour to meet the needs of all their pupils whether they are of the faith or not;

- Offer high standards of education;
- Work in partnership with other schools and organizations from the voluntary and statutory sectors . . .
- (in the case of faith schools), nurture young people in the faith of their family. (DCSF, 2007: 7)

Whether the above bullet points are indeed possible relate to the issues which have been examined in this chapter. The history of faith schools involves different faith groupings investing in education, the evolution of state sponsored alternatives for faith schools and a recent trend of expansion of faith schools with more denominations being encouraged to open new schools. However, the evidence suggests that Christian churches have monopolized this development *so far* in England. As Walford (2008: 694) explains: 'It is worth noting that none of the 83 Academies is sponsored by a non-Christian faith group'. Education policy evidence calls for a more inclusive education policy which reflects the general education policy trend of opening education to different denominations in England and Wales (DfEE, 2001; DfES, 2002; DCSF, 2007). Flint (2007: 265) offers one argument and suggests, society and culture needs more, '. . . civic partnership, which will necessarily include ethnicity and religion, framed within a secular legal citizenship and responsible to evolving local contexts'. This implies greater community cohesion and the potential for more multi-faith schooling. The respondents who were questioned in relation to faith and multi-faith schooling also raised significant issues. The interviewee below – a university lecturer – taught religious education in a state-maintained school and is reflecting on past practice:

University Lecturer – For me, it very much was, and I should say there are many different concepts of religious education now perhaps which have moved away from that. It has been sometime since I taught religious education in secondary schools but that's what certainly interested me, but also this idea that if education is about reflecting on yourself or drawing upon yourself, it seems a multicultural approach gives that. For me, the concern is, and I can see it in government policies and also new approaches by teachers themselves who want to see everything as neatly packaged pieces of knowledge which you don't transmit from yourselves standing by the interactive whiteboard to the child. I can see how multiculturalism doesn't fit into that because you need to make everything simple and these are the way things are. For me the interest of the multicultural approach and education seems to be one and the same.

Those 'neatly packaged pieces of knowledge' which combine with the league table requirements seem to quantify education which focuses on success (DfES, 2002; Troman et al., 2007; Nicholl and McClellan, 2008; Goldstein, 2008) rather than avoid the education focus on cultural and faith difference. This seems to miss the complicated issues of cultural diversity that different faith communities bring to schools, society and education systems (Banks, 2006). A greater multi-faith curriculum which involves and includes children in debates across many education subjects for example, citizenship, history, addresses issues of diversity (Banks, 2009). This reflects what Jackson (2006: 54) describes as '... an analysis of plurality that incorporates both "traditional" aspects, such as overt religious diversity, and "modern" elements, such as competing rationalities and epistemologies and interpersonal contact enhanced by new technology'.

Different ideas can be exchanged in schools within virtual environments, which in this case mean's using the world wide web as a tool when teaching cultural difference in the classroom or / and lecture theatre (Livingstone, 2009). This can be applicable to both modern elements and traditional aspects of faith and multi-faith schooling. Parsons (2008: 402) offers a potential solution for the expansion of multi-faith schooling which focuses on multiculturalism and education. 'Multicultural education has long worked at promoting the use of examples and artefacts from minority ethnic groups; it has championed multi faith worship and direct experience of other ethnicities in the school.' Parsons suggests possible interpersonal solutions for faith organizations to help minority communities. This can depend on the school's mission (Grace, 2003) but the issue addresses social and cultural issues that concern all schools which potential leads to greater community cohesion (Cantle, 2008).

Reflective Exercise

Questions taken from Gardner (in Gardner et al., 2005: 9)

- To what extent can faith communities in their state-sponsored schools set about answering [multi faith] questions . . . according to their own dispositions and preferences?
- Should they not also respond to them against criteria embedded in the boundaries of inclusiveness and multiple identities which both implicitly and explicitly underpin and shape the purpose of our current general state education?

Summary

Cultural identities are shaped by how we perceive ourselves, but significantly also as how others perceive us. As Banks and Banks (2007: 74) explain: 'Identity formation is key to the cultural coherence argument. Possessing a clear and coherent identity does not come about without the aid of exterior influences. An identity is always relational and comparative to others'. This suggests a conditional 'two-way' relationship, as was discussed in Chapter 2 of this book, when the integration concept was examined. When reflecting on multiculturalism and faith, a teacher trainee reacts below to a question on whether faith schools can indeed have a multi-faith focus with the following comment:

> Interviewee – Being realistic, well of course they should. But then would becoming more multicultural mean losing the identity which is associated with their faith?

Faith school communities with long histories, not just in England, are not prepared to lose their identities, either through state-funding or co-funding partnerships. The counter argument to this is that faith schools should be more multicultural and focus on other community identities and cohesion (Cantle, 2008). Another argument tends to suggest that faith based education needs to go beyond these issues to increase understanding and knowledge *within and between* faiths. This can potentially come through a more multi-faith curricula which deals with different beliefs within different subjects that is, religious studies, history and citizenship. Taking these arguments forward into the next chapter, we will extend the conceptual debate in the final two chapters to the subject of citizenship and whether educationally, it can allow the conditions and possibilities of a more multi-faith education and systems of schooling.

Useful websites

Centre for Research and Evaluation in Muslim Education (CRÈME)
  www.ioe.ac.uk/research/75205.html
The Catholic Church in England and Wales
  www.catholic-ew.org.uk/
The Church of England
  www.cofé.anglican.org/
Religion
  www.bbc.co.uk/religion/
Religious Education
  www.coxhoe.durham.sch.uk/Curriculum/RE.htm

Multiculturalism and Education 5

Introduction

Multiculturalism and education are both contemporary and connected with a number of factors addressed in this book so far. In previous chapters we have looked at concepts and ideas, such as multiculturalism, integration and segregation which have shaped education policy. We have also looked at how issues which concern faith schools shape education curricula, culture and the societies that we live in. We now move on to empirical data based on questionnaires and interviews that highlight debates concerning multiculturalism and education. When examining the past and present of multicultural education, the first section of this chapter analyses multicultural education experiences taken from respondents who were questioned and interviewed for this book. The issue of the compatibility of multiculturalism within education is also addressed. Then we examine whether it is possible to advance the concept of multiculturalism within a post 7/7 world (Eade et al., 2008). The chapter ends with a conceptual examination of the future of multiculturalism within ongoing educational debates.

Past and present: multicultural education experiences

This section examines responses to three main issues in relation to multiculturalism and education. It draws first on the personal educational experiences of multiculturalism. Secondly, it addresses the practice of individuals within the education profession. Thirdly, it examines whether multiculturalism as a concept was or is compatible within educational contexts. A combination of university lecturers, undergraduate and postgraduate students, teacher trainers and trainees, as well as individuals who are involved within interest groups concerning multiculturalism and education, give domestic and international insights into how people perceive different aspects of multiculturalism and education. The first example is based on a university lecturer's reflections in interview on a situation concerning a social and cultural situation which touched upon different communities in Vancouver, Canada:

> *University Lecturer – . . . lots of immigrants came to Canada and a government policy [was created] to try and deal with the different cultures that make up Canada. [I'm] not sure what all the ins and outs comparing it with the UK policy are but the aims are quite similar in that you have different cultures that can keep their cultural identities, traditions, language . . . Some government money is made available, as it is in the UK, for programmes and cultural sectors and those types of things. Initially, I think it is an important aspect of Canadian identity . . . But there comes a point where these cultures and a way of life in whatever country [e.g.] the UK or Canada, do come head on and one example, a Canadian example . . . a few years ago a group of Iranians who were living in Vancouver came as immigrants, refugees. [They] . . . petitioned the council in North Vancouver to segregate the public swimming pool – an area for women and an area for men. They wanted to segregate the public pool, public facilities and it went to the local council and the council said no because it went against the ethos of Canadian society . . . So there can be a point where yes, diversity, but it cannot come head on to the*

*existing way of thinking and traditions and those sorts of things. How
do you tolerate the intolerable? Can you tolerate the intolerable?*
Interviewer – The intolerable being?
*University Lecturer – The intolerable being if you assume that it's a demo-
cratic, liberal society and then you have ideas that cannot fit within
or do not want to fit within a country.*

Canada, as was described in the first chapter of this book, was the first country in the world to create an official multicultural policy and it has evolved over time but there will always be tensions within a country concerning cultural diversity. The Iranian community in North Vancouver attempted to 'interact and participate' (Phillips, 2005) with the majority culture but they were refused segregated access to a swimming pool. The Iranian community could have been potentially granted segregated access for one afternoon or evening per week to the swimming pool. The minority came up against the majority, in this case an example of the 'intolerable being' highlighted by the interviewee above, and were refused segregated access which gives insights into both integrationist and multicultural policy in Canada. This above exam-ple highlights how the two-way process of integration suggests that conditions can be set within a political decision by the state and majority community.

Reflective Exercise

- Should the Iranians have been granted access to the swimming pool? Should or could a compromise have been reached in North Vancouver?

When considering teachers' multicultural education experiences, several respondents underlined the need to continually develop teachers to deliver more multicultural education in the classroom and lecture theatre (Ramsey, 2004; Banks, 2009). That opinion is expressed by a university teacher trainer who worked in Birmingham as a secondary school teacher in the 1980s. She worked in both pre- and post-Swann (DES, 1985) eras – see Chapter 2 – so that information contextualizes the viewpoints below:

*Interviewer – There was tension between minority communities in 2005
in Birmingham [England] . . . (Interviewee – Indeed) . . . . So, that in
itself is an interesting development. Just after Phillips speech. Let's talk*

> *about Birmingham [England] and your experiences briefly. This notion of segregation, were communities segregated when you were teaching in the 1980s? How did you cope as a practitioner with the segregation in the school?*
>
> *University Teacher Trainer – With great difficulty. The solution centres on a strong belief in trying to help with the understanding between communities, the mutual beliefs and getting a feel for the communities. There was a lot of work going on to build communities but equally a lot of social segregation.*
>
> *Interviewer – How much support would you have gained from colleagues from the school, the local authority at that time?*
>
> *University Teacher Trainer – Quite a lot from colleagues who were actually on the ground within the school within a shared discussion, a shared purpose in what we were trying to achieve.*

The events in Birmingham in 2005 showed conflict between communities (Gereluk and Race, 2007) but we gain insights into the experiences of professional practitioners. The current university lecturer was finding it difficult to cope with segregation within Birmingham 30 years before the civic disturbances of 2005. However, a multicultural debate concerning education was taking place in England during the 1980s (DES, 1985). As the university teacher trainer above implies, more critical education practice relating to the issues concerning segregation and racism, rather than tokenistic interventions, are still required in contemporary education to deal with culturally diverse classrooms (Ramsey, 2004).

Education practice in multicultural environments

It is not *what* is taught in education but *how* subject material is taught within culturally diverse educational environments (Ramsey, 2004). The university lecturer below, in an interview, talks about pedagogy and specifically methods employed to deliver multicultural curricula during his time as an undergraduate student:

> *University Lecturer – . . . I attended a seminar on Cultural Theory and one of our lecturers . . . is a staunch Marxist and the way that he put his view across was not dogmatic. He could have been. We were all*

there waiting to be preached to, but he didn't do that and he set
about deconstructing his own case. It was incredibly humbling,
watching this very intelligent person break off from what he was
saying go about deconstructing everything that he stood for and it
wasn't just a matter of argument, this was a method of faith as well.
He was willing to subject himself to that kind of inquiry.
Interviewer – So, it was the method and how it was taught?
University Lecturer – Yes, that was crucial and it made us think if he is
opening up himself to critically engage with his own perspective then
we should be able to do the same. So, that is one lesson, you lead
from the front in these kind of matters. That is one thing that sticks
over the years. That's the one thing I remember strongly.

Teaching methods are as important as content and it is how teachers are given opportunities to develop their practice which matters, concerning how students debate, digest and form their own opinions. Using Watkins and Mortimore's (1999: 3) definition of pedagogy as: 'any conscious activity by one person designed to enhance learning in another', the impact on teaching and learning has to be productive for all concerned in the classroom. Continuing professional development allows practitioners to reflect on experiences and develop good practice. The interviewee below – a university teacher trainer – gives insights into how she approaches issues concerning multiculturalism:

Interviewer – Can you give examples of getting people into teaching who
may have more experience . . .
University Teacher Trainer – I come from a science background, so national
curriculum Science [when the national curriculum was introduced in
England and Wales in 1988] – I was up there. Banging on tambou-
rines, saying we need science, doing work on diversity [and] multi-
culturalism and again trying to get that message across to other
practitioners. It didn't fit, it wasn't supposed to and if it was, 'I don't
know what you mean?' We've got the picture of the black child in
here, we've got something about their culture. What do you mean?
We are not being multicultural about the way we are teaching. You
want me to talk about different coloured skin? You want me to look
at people, diversity of eye colour and whatever? Yes, ok we've talked
about how people have different coloured skin, we've even made
different colours from different coloured paint and talked about the
science of that. But what is not done there is surface level analysis.
There is nothing underneath it to give it any weight or understanding.

> *There is no encouragement of understanding; it's pulling up differences [Interviewer – Superficial?] Yes, very superficial and very . . . I think it makes things more segregated. There was a big buzz thing going on around when I was an Advisory Teacher for Primary Science. What you should be doing is looking for the similarities and celebrating the differences. Wonderful ethos if done in a particular way . . .*
>
> *Interviewer – That's Swann philosophy essentially. That's what he was saying.*
>
> *University Teacher Trainer – But there is a massive difference between celebrating the difference and really believing in it and that whole ethos you promote as a person to your own understanding and doing the surface bit which is delivering what you are supposed to be delivering without the understanding beneath it.*
>
> *Interviewer – Good practice?*
>
> *University Teacher Trainer – Good practice taken from people just exploring ideas I think, given time, given space to develop understanding. Taking a starting point as where people actually are, so it takes away the value issue before you start, so that you are not automatically tub thumping about what should happen and how people should feel and how people should understand.*
>
> *Interviewer – Using evidence constructively, you are not trying to make one point, you are making several . . .*
>
> *University Teacher Trainer – Yes, and I think very much starting from beliefs and understanding without making judgements. So, you are not judging people as being right or wrong in their judgements before they start.*

The university teacher trainer above gives examples of how practice needs to go beyond the superficial to increase understandings of cultural diversity within education environments. Again, the notion of the tokenistic is implied when considering how diverse practice is or is not within the classroom. Exploring different ideas needs to be encouraged, but having the time to do so, rather than teaching to a test in English, as well as other international contexts, is a continuing contemporary education issue. Being impartial is also recognized and continuing professional development (Burton and Bartlett, 2005) would be a productive opportunity to reflect upon and examine professional practice. Issues concerning multiculturalism, racism and discrimination can be addressed. This is highlighted in interview by a university lecturer below:

Interviewer – Can you give examples of present multicultural practice?

University Lecturer – We are talking about difference? Ok, in relation to disability, at the same time we apply this to racism, to multiculturalism. So, we try to draw the parallels. And we bring in examples in relation to discrimination on the basis of racism in much the same way we talk about discrimination of disability. However, I can give you more examples from schools here in the UK and what we used to do in Greek schools . . . for instance, Teleconferences by children are supposed to communicate with children in other schools across Europe or other countries in order to get to know each other. In order to explore their similarities and also to talk about their differences and to get to know each other so as to respect difference.

All professional practitioners need to be provided with opportunities to not only reflect on practice, but also encouraged to learn new methods and techniques such as applying comparative examples through teleconferences with the consequent benefit of children being able to communicate not just across Europe but the world. A great deal here depends upon school expenditure and resources to allow a practice like this to take place. However, any opportunity to explore similarities and differences which will possibly increase knowledge and understanding of difference has to be promoted in all educational contexts. Comparative method – which is the application of similarities and differences of international examples to domestic contexts (Phillips and Schweisfurth, 2007) – can be used to promote a more global outlook (Lechner, 2009; Ritzer; 2010). Moreover, comparative method can be employed in continuing professional development courses to avoid the scenario expressed by a university teacher trainer below:

Interviewer – Can you give examples of present or past multicultural practice in the classroom or lecture theatre?

University Teacher Trainer – A few months ago, I went to and sat next to . . . a girl in the classroom and obviously there was something wrong and the girl who sat next to us said: 'She's Korean. She's Korean; you can't do anything with her'.

Interviewer – She's almost been labelled and dismissed.

University Teacher Trainer – And I said, wait a minute, immediately, as a teacher that was a signal. I've got to do extra work or something has to happen here. And then the teacher's comment at the end of the lesson is: 'Oh don't worry, she'll get it in the end.' I didn't know what that really meant or what she was talking about . . .

Interviewer – . . . grasp the mathematical concepts of adding or subtracting.

University Teacher Trainer – . . . these children require more support. And so within the working environment for teachers, ok that might be too much for them, so they have to do something else . . . And so when the end is, I don't know what that means. End of 'what' in terms of her education?

Interviewer – How does a teacher address an issue like that in a class of 20 students? It can be very difficult.

University Teacher Trainer – There are more teaching assistants, so there is something there that could be used to benefit [these] children far more and who are obviously dedicated in mathematics. There should be no problem having teaching assistants in Korean or whatever it maybe. Why not? And they should be put into the school for certain because I think it might be the best way of addressing the issue to help these children to progress.

There is an example in the above data of how a child is immediately labelled because of her cultural identity. As the university teacher trainer above highlights: 'She'll get it in the end', is not a good enough response. The teacher needed to do more and a discussion took place between teacher trainer and teacher trainee after the lesson. This is a very complex scenario, although a classroom assistant, if in attendance could have possibly helped. But the teacher trainer highlights that teaching assistants should be bilingual, in this case Korean, to help both the teacher and the child. However, if a teaching assistant were in that classroom and did not know the Korean language, the student would still have difficulties understanding maths. So practical assistance in the classroom needs to be combined with what is actually taught in different education environments.

Reflective Exercise

- What new pedagogical methods can be promoted to encourage the teaching of similarities and differences that is, the comparative method?

The compatibility of multiculturalism and education

Respondents were asked within the questionnaires and interviews whether they believed multiculturalism as a concept was or is compatible with education. The interviewee who worked in a multicultural interest group addresses this issue below:

> *Interviewee – I think yes, because through education you can celebrate difference and it is within schools that children are supposed to learn how to respect, not only tolerate but also respect difference and therefore schools have a major role to play in promoting multi-culturalism. And we have many, many examples of schools trying to actually cultivate the feeling of multiculturalism and bringing children together in order to explore differences and at the same time to acknowledge the fact that similarities outweigh differences. Yes, in schools from my experience, they organise celebrations and festivals in order to make evident the fact that we are different and it is necessary to respect difference.*
>
> *Interviewer – Was this the case . . . through your own practical experiences?*
>
> *Interviewee – . . . we are talking about multiculturalism during the last few years . . . So, now yes. There is a lot of debate around the necessity to promote multiculturalism in schools, something that was not the case some years ago. However . . . things are very differ-ent because we have a strong feeling of our . . . identity. And due to historical reasons, we try in different ways and in many ways to promote and in a way protect our national identity.*

Issues concerning multiculturalism still have to compete with a national identity being 'protected' so there is a clash of interest here between majority and minority communities. This can be seen as another application of the conditional two-way integrationist policy argument which was developed in Chapter 2 whereby the state promotes and protects national identity. Both this application and the interviewee's comments above can be challenged when reflecting on British and European identities (Aughey, 2007; Geddes, 2008). The final two comments in this section from interviews, the first from a uni-versity teacher trainer, the second from a teacher trainee, also reflect on the issue of the compatibility of education and multiculturalism.

University Teacher Trainer – Well, every class is a multicultural experience really . . . Even if you hold religious beliefs you have to put that to one side and have to look at that objectively. And you have to look at it critically and explore how it works. The kind of moments where I have felt like there has been a mutual understanding – I taught a class and listening to some of the students . . . they did a session on religious beliefs that they all held. The first aim was getting them to talk to each other about their attitudes to their own religions. The second aim was getting students talking of the kind of aspects of religion that are meaningful to them and be able to reflect on that to the rest of the class which was ultimately a very good multicultural experience. But that's an advanced version of what I was saying [about] primary and secondary education. I mean, that's articulating quite directly . . . multiculturalism.

Teacher Trainee – I think multicultural practice is not just about one scenario. I think it's about everything you do. It's about what ethos you provide and promote from the point of children. Do they feel located as a community? Are their needs met within the community? Can they access the curriculum? Can they access distinct examples of what is multicultural practice? I think it's about the whole learning and teaching environment that raises questions about: How do you engage the whole community? Because good multicultural practice is about everybody, it's not about one particular set of views or the other. It's about actually raising questions that support everyone's learning.

The evidence above suggests that the majority of educational experiences are multicultural. However, these experiences depend upon how they are acknowledged and how teachers and students understand the experience. This relates in one way to a multi-faith base, where a plurality of beliefs are expressed and taught, as the university teacher trainer above suggests, but also enshrines a whole pedagogical philosophy relating to multiculturalism as the teacher trainee underlines. Multicultural education includes acknowledging and including not just the child or student, but also the family, the local community and learning and teaching environments which relates to levels of engagement within a community (Cantle, 2008; Banks, 2009).

Reflective Exercise

- Can all educational experiences be multicultural?
- Can we have a multicultural pedagogy?

Has multiculturalism been replaced with another social construction?

What was interesting in co-editing Eade et al. (2008), a book which attempts to advance the concept of multiculturalism, was how far the concept of integration had influenced social policy in many countries, not just England. The chapters by Kumar, Modood and Johnson and Verlot, in Eade et al. (2008) made the writing of the introduction of that book particularly challenging when, as the title suggested, the editors were attempting to advance the concept of multiculturalism (Race in Eade et al., 2008a). The focus of those three chapters was on integration. Eade et al. (2008) aimed to continue the ongoing debate about the concepts of multiculturalism and integration. One issue which was examined centred on whether 7/7 was influenced by integrationist or multicultural social and education policy (Race in Eade et al., 2008a: 2; Race, 2009b). Banks (2009) also continues the debates concerning the conceptual examination of multiculturalism and education. The evidence presented in this section examines whether multiculturalism as a concept had been replaced with another social construction.

As Gergen and Gergen (2009: 816) argue, 'The phase social construction typically refers to a tradition of scholarship that traces the origin of knowledge and meaning and the nature of reality to processes generated within human relationships'. In relation to whether multiculturalism as a concept had been replaced by another social construction, the first respondent – a university lecturer – suggests multiculturalism has been replaced by a concept of multi-identity:

> *University Lecturer – What is it to be British? What is British identity? We have the exact same thing in Canada being next door to huge neighbours and what is our identity? What is Canadian identity? And then as a person coming here [to England]: Who am I? . . . And I think the struggle of wanting to come up with this identity in some respects has taken over the multicultural emphasis.*

The issue of multi-identity here concerns majority and minority communities and how individuals and communities perceive their identities and identity in contemporary society (du Gay, 2007; Elliot and du Gay, 2009). The issue of multi-identity for the interviewee highlights the complexity of the assimilation, integration and multicultural conceptual debate highlighted in Chapter 2. The individual in the above scenario has the choice of assimilating into a new identity, keeping the old and taking on new aspects of a new countries identity within an integrationist model, or acknowledging and celebrating all identities within a multicultural framework. Preserving an old identity, choosing a new identity or having a multi-identity which is possible within integrationist and multicultural conceptual modules is the dilemma and 'struggle' the interviewee recognizes (Eade et al., 2008). The next interviewee – a postgraduate student – underlines the advances of multiculturalism and cultural diversity in London and goes as far as recognizing the city as a melting pot. That image was both analysed and criticized in Chapter 2 as immigrants lost part of their identity within a one-way processes of assimilation or the two-way process of integration:

> *Interviewer – Has [multiculturalism] been conceptually replaced?*
> *Postgraduate Student – There are really two answers to that when I look at my friends living in London, in the inner city, I can see the incredible strides forward we have made since I was young and growing up.*
> *Interviewer – Do you think cultural diversity is more recognised now then it was 30 years ago?*
> *Postgraduate Student – Most definitely with all the people that I see on the street, it might be just my friendship group, but I think I've got a fairly diverse range of friends, but although they would still celebrate difference, there is that difference. People come together and there are the hybridisations that come between Indian youth into the Ragga music. There are all kinds of mixtures. There is much more respect on the street amongst peoples than there used to be.*
> *Interviewer – Is that melting pot metaphor healthy?*
> *Postgraduate Student – I would personally like to think it is . . . I've got a strong link into different communities. I think it is a wonderful thing and that's part of the reason I live in London. I regard it as a great world city. So, I think it is, but I just think we need to work on it . . . I think that is very difficult.*

The postgraduate student's notion of the melting-pot was questioned in the first chapter of this book because although living anywhere within and among different communities is advantageous when considering cultural diversity, it is also what is lost within the melting-pot metaphor when thinking of assimilation and integration which needs to be considered. This consideration relates to the notion of community cohesion (HO, 2001; Cantle, 2008) raised earlier in the book and what can be gained through a greater acknowledgement of cultural diversity, through the difficulties highlighted by the interviewee above. The postgraduate student is attempting to highlight the importance of diverse communities but misinterprets the melting-pot metaphor. This is one of the many reasons why a multicultural focus is still important and worth advancing today (Eade et al., 2008).

Reflective Exercise

- Are cities more cultural diverse today than they were ten years ago?
- What brings communities together and makes them cohesive?

Is multiculturalism worth advancing? Is it healthy as a concept?

The first two comments from a university teacher trainer and university lecturer in this section focus on aspects of multicultural education and whether the concept in an educational context is worth pursuing:

> University Teacher Trainer – It all depends upon the person doing the teaching because we have all got our own prejudices and I think with some people, it comes across, and with others you know they are being open and honest. With other people, you just walk into a room and you feel it. The atmosphere changes. They've judged you by just walking into a room . . . it's happened to me many times and depending what mood I'm in I just go with the flow and if they want to treat me that way, that's fine. Other times, I'll stand up for my rights, I'm able to advocate for myself and I do it on a daily basis for people, young people but that's why I say it can depend on the teacher . . .
>
> University Lecturer – I think as an Asian male, the number of teachers with ethnic backgrounds is pitiful. If you . . . look at the numbers of teaching staff and the diversity of the student body compared to the members of staff, there is just no comparison. So, that's a problem. That's one way if you are looking to advance an understanding of different cultures and there is a relationship between your background and your ability to look upon the world in a different way.

Neither respondent directly claims multiculturalism is worth advancing but the implication from the university teacher trainer suggests that the teacher 'doing the teaching' can produce an atmosphere in which diversity, not multicultural issues can be discussed. The potential of a focus on both diversity and multicultural issues is examined in the next chapter with analysis of the subject of citizenship within education. The university lecturer above reflects on the number, or lack of teachers, from ethnic minority backgrounds in education. The background and attitude of a teacher can influence what is being taught to an audience. Continuing professional development can be used as a vehicle for practitioners to reflect on issues that concern cultural diversity. The interviewee below – an individual involved in a multicultural interest group – examines the need for that focus on diversity:

> *Interviewer – Is there a difference between diversity and multiculturalism do you think?*
>
> *Interviewee – Yes, I don't think in practice there is a big gap between them. Conceptually, there is a gap. Diversity is, I suppose, about understanding preference and individual preference. And multiculturalism acknowledges cultures if you like, traditions, backgrounds and family values whatever these things are, although I think people have very different ways of thinking about multiculturalism.*
>
> *Interviewer . . . What do you think about multiculturalism?*
>
> *Interviewee – I think of it as a mixture of recognising many cultures but that can mean different things. It's not just about ethnicity, it's about family background, about your local area for instance and how that affects you. There are a lot of other things that might shape you.*

The above comments are significant as we can see how a term such as diversity in the 1990s and 2000s became in England as significant as multiculturalism had been in the 1970s and 1980s (Griffiths, 2003). A comparison between diversity and multiculturalism is made and the interviewee claims diversity is about personal preference while multiculturalism is a more encompassing idea which addresses culture, ethnicity, family and the locality. That in itself implies that the concept of multiculturalism is still relevant and has more than something to offer on debates surrounding issues that is, social justice and inclusion. The comment below from a university lecturer analyses how healthy the concept or label of multiculturalism is:

> *University Lecturer – Well, what I feel strongly is that multiculturalism has never been meaningful at schools and needs to be meaningful . . .*
> *I think that is exactly right with what is going on in schools as parents*

are being invited to come in and show children how to cook different foods and things like this, none of which is made meaningful to the children apart from the fact that they are experiencing different cooking which might have happened when I was at school. But I think it has a very limited benefit . . . The issues at stake are not really being brought to the foreground . . . So, I think that those issues are much more critical and meaningful to look at in terms of what multiculturalism might actually mean. I think this would be useful.

Multiculturalism has never, for the university lecturer above, had meaning in schools and is therefore criticized. This goes beyond a conceptual definition and analysis – see Chapter 1 – towards the practical application and meaning of cooking foods from different continents which in the interviewee's eyes does not go far enough. More information is needed on the background of that country, as well as the need to stimulate debates on other issues for example, the economic comparison of the export and import of foods. As Ramsey (2004) implies, the practical application of multiculturalism has to have meaning within different teaching and learning contexts.

Does multiculturalism have a future?

Even though there are continuing debates about advancing the concept of multiculturalism (Eade et al., 2008), what follows suggests that whatever is thought or said, the conceptual debate surrounding multiculturalism will continue. The first interviewee – a university teacher trainer – in this section puts across simple yet crucial issues that concern multiculturalism and cultural diversity. The first response focuses on increasing understanding of multiculturalism.

Interviewer – Does multiculturalism have a future?

University Lecturer – Well, it has a future if we approach it . . . we do have to, the first way is to get to understanding of the term which is incredibly important.

Interviewer – And very difficult?

University Lecturer – Yes, I've experienced living in different countries in the world and living in . . . groups and hearing some really awful things from . . . groups towards different cultures. It's just unhealthy living and the only reason these comments were made was a lack of understanding.

The next respondent – a university lecturer – also focuses on 'what schools can do' in relation to multicultural education.

> *University Lecturer – Multiculturalism is a big question. Multiculture is always going to be a . . . social fact . . . To that extent, we need to ensure that cultures are respected, forms of solidarity are created . . . and the forms of and the role culture plays in sustaining those needs some kind of recognition by government. It comes top down and goes through institutions . . . and schools too. But whether in its existing forms it has to be kept alive, I probably think not . . . I think there needs to be a lot of work in trying to decouple multiculture from race and faith and looking at culture in terms of what we experience . . . of what schools do.*

If the concept of multiculturalism is dead as Phillips (2005) suggests, it could theoretically be replaced by a term like multiculture . However, the above interviewee suggests that whatever term is used, it needs to be separated from issues such as race, racism and faith schools to allow a bigger picture viewpoint of the complexity of issues that concern multicultural education. When considering advancing the debate of multicultural education (Banks, 2009), a postgraduate student and university lecturer who was interviewed, has an interesting idea and education focus:

> *Interviewee – I think one way we could do that is by listening to our students. Right from the very start not necessarily producing for them . . . this might be a bit utopian, I'm not sure how it would work in practice but you talk to the students about issues which are important and what engages them with the real world, so perhaps you would have to think on your feet . . . it would mean a lot of work but students should have the chance to say what happened on the news last night. We need to encourage the sort of notion of an active citizenship. I think we need to go right back to basics in our pedagogy and include students within it, making special care not necessarily to listen to the loudest and most eloquent voices.*

The issue of pedagogy becoming more focused on students, so as to understand what is going on and changing, within our cultures is a constructive idea. Students are as aware of wide-ranging issues and should theoretically be given the opportunity to articulate their ideas (Leach, 2009; Wells, 2009). Multicultural education (Banks, 2009) continues to focus on the student voice. If culture and multiculture continues to change within continuing globalization then perhaps we need to not only understand the history of how education curriculum was shaped and formed (Aldrich, 2002) but we need to also rethink it (White, 2004) to make schooling at all levels of education more relevant to students and teachers. And that claim is underlined by a university teacher trainer below which supports multiculturalism as an idea, but is critical of what is taught in education:

> *University Teacher Trainer – . . . [multiculturalism] is fundamental . . . I think what we have tended to skip over within the general focus on standards in schools . . . is an engagement with issues about values and learning about the world and how we live. And unfortunately, the contemporary curriculum is more a collection of assembled subjects and effective teaching and a whole school approach does promote the discussion of debates on values and ethics and all sorts of those issues. The difficulty though remains that multiculturalism is not a central curriculum strand, and so what happens is that there is some multicultural discussion, but the emphasis isn't necessarily put on perhaps locating learning strongly enough in those sorts of debates relating to the following questions: Why do we need to be tolerant? Why do we need to understand different positions? I think it is there in the curriculum but it's not there in depth.*

Something *more* is required to understand different positions, issues and questions. The interviewee above argues that multiculturalism cannot provide this as it is not central within the national curriculum in England. Where that focus could come from in education is addressed in the next chapter when we examine the potential of the citizenship curriculum.

Reflective Exercise

- Is ' . . . more of the same enough . . . ' for students in education or does ' . . . more need to be done . . . ' when thinking of multiculturalism and cultural diversity?

Summary

In many respects, this chapter has confirmed a great deal of the arguments that were put forward in Eade et al., (2008). It was argued in that text by different authors that the concept of multiculturalism, at the very least, needed continuing debate and revision when applying it in education to contemporary, domestic and international contexts (Harty and Murphy, 2005; Pang et al., 2006; Race, 2009a). The compatibility of multiculturalism and education is based upon what is taught in education curricula. What information is not chosen to be taught and who are or are not accommodated means that children can possibly be excluded and segregated (Ball, 2003; Archer and Francis, 2007; Banks, 2009). Multicultural education practice, to be more effective, developed from the data collected for this book, and highlighted in this chapter, needs to depend on:

- Method – how practice allows students to talk, think and reflect;
- Depth – practice needs to avoid the tokenistic. Stereotyping needs to be avoided at all costs;
- Reach – practice needs to be international rather than national.

Chapters in Eade et al. (2008; CIC, 2007) implied that integration had replaced multiculturalism within the conceptual debate concerning cultural diversity although this is in itself is debatable (Giddens, 2007; Modood, 2007). Some of the interviewee comments highlighted in this chapter focused on the possibility of a conceptual replacement or improvement of multiculturalism. In relation to the health of multicultural education, comments from the data were mixed concerning different interpretations and perceptions. Method was important as to how and who was teaching what in the classroom. Other concepts and issues such as diversity and inequality needed to be focused upon and were viewed as practically more meaningful than multiculturalism. It was agreed by the majority of respondents that multiculturalism had a conceptual future and one avenue where this could happen was through citizenship education. That is an issue which will be addressed in the penultimate and final chapters of this book, which will focus on the potential of the concepts of citizenship (Pattie et al., 2004; Lister and Pia, 2008; Somers, 2008) and citizenship education (HoC, 2007).

Useful website

James. A. Banks homepage

   www.faculty.washington.edu/jbanks/MESeries.htm

The Glossary of Education Reform – Multicultural Education

   www.edglossary.org/multicultural-education/

The Potential of Citizenship When Reflecting on Multiculturalism and Education

6

Introduction

In this final chapter, the aim is to address several issues that promote and advance multiculturalism and education (Eade et al., 2008; Race, 2009c). The concept of citizenship and its introduction, implementation and revision within the education curriculum of England and Wales is highlighted (QCA, 1998; DfES, 2006; 2007). The potential of the current citizenship curricula needs to be analysed by looking at content from the Qualifications and Curriculum Development Agency (QCDA, 2009a; 2009b). The role of teachers concerning multicultural education relating to cultural diversity highlights the need for continuing professional development to raise awareness over issues of diverse classrooms. The conceptual debate will also continue with discussions on how useful Critical Race Theory (CRT) and interculturalism are when debating the issues surrounding topics that is, racism and cultural diversity that develop the equality and equal opportunities remit of multiculturalism. This chapter ends with reflections on multiculturalism and education and the ongoing debates which focus on elements of social and cultural diversity.

The ongoing conceptual debate – citizenship

The concept of citizenship within the national curriculum of England and Wales has a recent history. It was only introduced into the National Curriculum in 2002 and was only then statutory at Key Stages 3 and 4 (for those children aged 11–16) and non-statutory at Key Stages 1 and 2 (for those children aged 5–11). To put citizenship as a concept relating to education into context, we have to examine the role of Bernard Crick (QCA: 1998) who was influential in the promotion of citizenship but not in the creation of the citizenship curriculum.

Crick (2008) acknowledged that the 7/7 attacks on London changed the original National Curriculum for citizenship. Crick (1990: 1–18) defined himself as a 'moderate socialist' and believed in a citizenship focus within education but also recognized how education could be shaped by politics. He also believed that cultural learning should not be the monopoly of traditional education environments for example, schools. Crick believed that change would come through education. In his capacity as a lecturer at Sheffield University in England, he tutored David Blunkett, (1995: 86–88) who would go on to be Education Secretary in the Department for Education and Employment during Tony Blair's first term as prime minister (1997–2001). During that time, Blunkett, promoted the idea of citizenship in education, the first major subject introduction concerning the National Curriculum since 1988. It is worth looking at how the QCA, a committee appointed by Blunkett and chaired by Crick, defined in three points '. . . effective education for citizenship':

- Firstly, children learning from the very beginning self-confidence and socially and morally responsible behaviour both in and beyond the classroom, both towards those in authority and towards each other.
- Secondly, learning about and becoming helpfully involved in the life and concerns of their communities, including learning through community involvement and service to the community.

- Thirdly, pupils learning about and how to make themselves effective in public life through knowledge, skills and values. (QCA: 1998: 11–12)

Children's behaviour, community involvement and how pupils can make themselves 'effective' in public life can be viewed as a citizen's responsibility which is connected with learning in the school (Osler and Starkey, 2005). The term 'responsible' is again visible and we have seen in the second chapter of this book how this was used and interpreted in earlier education policy documentation (DES, 1971). Educational responsibility for underachievement at that time was focused on the child and the parent rather than the education system. As Armstrong explains, the term 'responsible' has a strong link with civic duty:

> Duty of responsibility has been a key term of citizenship throughout its history; the identity of the citizen is substantially constituted in terms of her (or more usually his) citizenly duties. Such duties have been interpreted in a whole host of different ways: the duty to bear arms, to dig for victory, to participate politically, to engage in cultural life and democratic dialogue, to support the state financially, to preserve the language or traditions of one's community, to reproduce and educate the citizens of the future, to respect the duties of civility, reasonableness, or industry. (Armstrong, 2006: 98)

According to Armstrong (ibid.), duty is an important component of citizenship, but so is engagement in 'cultural life' which raises an interesting connection with Trevor Phillips' speech highlighted in Chapter 3 of this book. Phillips was looking for communities to connect through an integrationist conceptual framework. An essential recommendation of the Crick Report was that '... citizenship education should be a statutory entitlement in the curriculum' (QCA, 1998: 22). The implication was that citizenship should be statutory and therefore compulsory at all key stages. The fact that citizenship would only be compulsory at Key Stages 3 and 4 raised a great deal of comment (McLaughlin, 2000; Heater, 2001; Olssen, 2004). Heater (2001: 119) suggests '... that change is more comfortable if it can be brought about gradually rather than speedily'. This perhaps explains why it took four years for a citizenship curriculum to be prepared for teaching in state-maintained schools in 2002. More significantly, Heater (2001: 120) also highlights that without '. . . a firm tradition of full government involvement places [a] greater strain on voluntary organizations . . . [and] teachers with perhaps little academic or professional background in the field'. Untrained teachers in the subject would find it difficult to actually prepare and teach citizenship. Olssen (2004) is critical of Crick (QCA: 1998) because 'effective education for citizenship takes into no account cultural difference', or the recommendations of the Runnymede Report which looked at the future of multi-ethnic Britain. As Parekh (2000: 302), Chair of the Runnymede Report argued: 'Education for citizenship should include human rights principles; stress on skills of deliberation, advocacy and campaigning; understanding of equality legislation; and opposition in racist beliefs and behaviour'. There is therefore a dual problem in relation to citizenship education: first, it would be difficult without a recognized subject history within education, to prepare and deliver a citizenship curriculum, secondly, the fact that the citizenship curriculum was not culturally diverse enough (Crick, 2008). Tyack raises another important point in relation to these problems:

> One assumes that civic unity is possible because people are basically alike, no matter what groups they may belong to (a variant of this approach holds that people may be initially quite different but are capable of becoming the same if properly instructed). (Tyack, 2003: 94–95)

The quote and Crick's (2008) views imply that citizenship could be perceived as a means of teaching civic unity to both majority and minority communities but the practical realities of teaching issues of cultural diversity are somewhat more complex than this implication.

Reflective Exercise

- How would you define 'effective education for citizenship'?
- Could citizenship education bring together contrasting points of views on cultural similarity and difference?

Diversity and citizenship

It is important to highlight the Ajegbo Report (DfES, 2007) which carried out a review of diversity and citizenship education in the National Curriculum in England. The review took place two years after the 7/7 London Bombings which allowed debates to take place in relation to integration, multiculturalism and citizenship (Eade et al., 2008; Osler, 2008). The report underlined an essential lack of cultural diversity being taught in schools. As Ajegbo himself wrote in the foreword:

> I believe issues around race, identity, citizenship and living together in the UK today are serious matters . . . I believe that schools, through their ethos, through their curriculum and through their work with their communities, can make a difference to those perceptions. (Ajegbo, DfES, 2007: 4–5)

Citizenship, because of events like 7/7, had become more educationally and politically important during the first decade of the twenty-first century. A concept like integration had within the creation of social policy become more important than multiculturalism (Phillips, 2005). As previous evidence in Chapter 2 has shown, policy documents like *Every Child Matters* were shaped within an integrationist conceptual framework (HO: 2003; DfES, 2004).

The first key finding of the Ajegbo (DfES, 2007: 6) report was that, 'the quality and quantity of education for diversity are uneven across England'. Therefore, issues such as cultural diversity were not being taught universally in state-maintained schools across the country. In relation to citizenship, the report found:

- Many teachers are unsure of the standard expected in Citizenship. This is not surprising, given that it is such a young statutory subject and that many teachers have no specific Citizenship training . . .
- Our Research Review found consensus among secondary headteachers and school staff that one of the biggest challenges to delivering Citizenship education was having being taught by non-specialists.
- Issues of identity and diversity are more often than not neglected in Citizenship education. When these issues are referred to, coverage is often unsatisfactory and lacks contextual depth.
- Much Citizenship education in secondary schools is not sufficiently contextualised for pupils to become interested and engaged with the local, national and international questions of the day and how politicians deal with them.
- Currently in Citizenship, issues of identity and diversity do not tend to be linked explicitly enough to political understanding (of legal and political systems) and active participation.
- The term 'British' means different things to different people. In addition, identities are typically constructed as multiple and plural. Throughout our consultations, concerns were expressed, however,

about defining 'Britishness', about the term's divisiveness and how it
can be used to exclude others. (DfES, 2007: 7–8)

Analysing the above points, many pre-2002 teachers are 'unsure' of citizenship
because they have not been taught how to teach the subject. That in itself is an
important observation because with the non-statutory nature of citizenship
education in primary schools, the number of citizenship teachers who would
have had the training or continuing professional development would have
been minimal (Murphy and Hall, 2008; Galton and MacBeath, 2008). More
teachers and specialists in citizenship were required. As the report acknowledges, coverage, meaning how the subject was taught and by whom, lacks not
only conceptual depth but teachers and students need to be engaged with relevant subject material. This lack of coverage also relates to issues like racism,
segregation and the need to understand the changing nature of cultural diversity. Recommendations, to address these issues, from the Ajegbo report (DfES,
2007) are highlighted below:

- Pupils Voice – All schools have mechanisms in place to ensure that the pupil
  voice is heard and acted upon. Schools should consider the use of forums, school
  councils, pupil questionnaires or other mechanisms for discussions around identity,
  values and belonging.
- Education for Diversity in the Curriculum – All schools should be encouraged to
  audit their curriculum to establish what they currently teach that is meaningful
  for all pupils in relation to diversity and multiple identities. The Qualifications and
  Curriculum Authority (QCA) 'Respect for All' is a useful audit tool. In the light of
  this audit, all schools should map provision across years and subjects and ensure
  that coverage is coherent.
- Harnessing local context – Schools should build active links between and across
  communities, with education for diversity as a focus:
  a. This might range from electronic links (local, national and global) to relationships
     through other schools (for example as part of a federation), links with busi-
     nesses, community groups and parents.
  b. These links should be encouraged particularly between predominately monocul-
     tural and multicultural schools.
  c. Such links need to be developed in such a way as to ensure they are sustainable.
  d. Such work between schools must have significant curriculum objectives and be
     incorporated into courses that pupils are studying. This will help avoid stereotyp-
     ing and tokenism. (DfES, 2007: 9–11)

Listening to what pupils and students have to say especially in relation to
identity or identities in the classroom is important because it raises the issue of

relevant curricula in relation to cultural diversity and multiculturalism. The issue of increasing student voice(s) was developed in the last chapter when considering promoting multicultural education. Changing the curriculum to make it 'meaningful' for all students highlights the previous point of promoting multicultural education in the sense that what is taught has to have contemporary relevance to the student. How citizenship is taught is also significant because this relates to teaching method and learning that is, pedagogy. Links with the local community are significant and build on existing legislation within the Education and Inspections Act (DfES, 2006) which called for more involvement by parents in schools and the joining of schools into federations. Beacon schools therefore theoretically offered subject centres of excellence and expertise in curriculum subjects. Multicultural links 'should be encouraged' which is fundamental to the message of this book because it implies that multicultural education should be promoted within the classroom (Banks, 2009).

This suggests that the concept of multiculturalism is still very much alive, as it is being mentioned and debated in the Ajegbo Report (DfES, 2007). This runs counter to the argument of Phillips (2005) who believed that multiculturalism as a concept is dead. Multicultural links need to be 'developed' by schools and not just in the sense of federations but links need to be developed within the community (Cantle, 2008). There are three more recommendations (DfES, 2007) that need to be examined at this point:

- Teacher Training – The Training and Development Agency for Schools (TDA) should evaluate the effectiveness of education for diversity across initial teacher training (ITT) providers.
- Citizenship – Given that the evidence suggests Citizenship education works best when delivered discretely, we recommend this as the preferred model for schools. We recommend greater definition and support in place of the flexible 'light touch' approach . . .
- Headteachers and senior management should prioritize whole-curriculum planning across the school and develop ways of linking Citizenship education effectively with other subjects, with the ethos of the schools, and with the community. (DfES, 2007: 9–11)

ITT is important within citizenship and diversity training should be given to this subject at all four Key Stages. 'Greater definition and support' is the required approach but this seems difficult when citizenship is a non-statutory subject within primary schools in England. For primary school teachers, a focus would be on the three core subjects of English, maths and science, not necessarily citizenship. The issue in relation to primary schools in England and citizenship education revolves around resources and whether schools can afford to deliver a citizenship curriculum that relates to a school when planning the whole curriculum rather than focusing on one subject.

There is no doubt the Ajegbo Report (DfES, 2007) did put forward an agenda for a revised citizenship education which encompassed more diversity and a revised focus on the concept of multiculturalism (Osler, 2009). The need for greater recognition of cultural diversity through citizenship education has also been promoted within international contexts (Banks, 2004). Interestingly, Alred et al. (2006) suggest that the concept of citizenship and citizenship education does not go far enough. They focus on an intercultural education and a global or cosmopolitan citizenship (Jackson, 2006; Gillborn 2008a; Osler, 2008). Hewitt (2005) addresses the development of citizenship education which should promote the capacity for autonomous thinking. Hewitt suggests that:

> Citizenship education not only involves promoting a certain sort of critical attitude towards authority, it also involved developing habits of civility and the capacity for public reasonableness. Both of these indirectly promote autonomy, since they encourage children to interact with the members of other groups, to understand the reasonableness of other ways of life, and to distance themselves from their own cultural traditions. (Hewitt, 2005: 308)

Interaction is crucial within citizenship education as majority and minority groups are encouraged to mix and learn from each other. However, autonomy suggests something a lot more individual and powerful then a respect for civil values. It should go beyond the notions of an integrationist, two-way relationship that is part of the community cohesion policy (Cantle, 2008). Hewitt continues:

> citizenship education typically has a dual function – it promotes a national identity within each constituent national group, defined by a common language and history, but it also seeks to promote some sort of transnational identity which can bind together the various national groups within the state. Unfortunately, recent developments . . . in states e.g. the breakdown of Yugoslavia and Czechoslovakia, the constitutional crises in Belgium and Canada – suggest that is very difficult to construct and maintain this transnational identity. (Hewitt, 2005: 214)

The fact that the promotion of a transnational identity, which Hewitt describes above as being difficult to teach, is in constant flux and continues to move with every migratory movement, has to be addressed to avoid what Hewitt (2005) describes in his research as a 'white backlash'. At the very least, the Ajegbo Report (DfES, 2007) has offered recommendations that can attempt through student voice, community involvement and continuing professional development, an agenda which can be theoretically addressed through citizenship, to produce and provide a more diverse education curriculum in England.

The potential of citizenship education

One of the main issues which was raised in the previous section was the potential of citizenship education for delivering a more inclusive, diverse and multicultural education. These issues do not only concern the English National Curriculum but have educational consequences for Europe (Keating, 2009) and other countries for example, Australia (Macintyre and Simpson, 2009). There is a potential, recognized within the Ajegbo report (DfES, 2007) of the Citizenship Curriculum, which can theoretically deliver a more focused curricula on cultural diversity. This potential will be examined by looking at elements of the Key Stage 4 of the Citizenship Curriculum (QCDA, 2009b) which is statutory and delivered to students aged 14–16 in secondary schools in England and Wales, focuses on the importance of the concept of citizenship. As a statutory subject, Key Stage 4 has more potential to include inclusive issues that concern citizenship and multiculturalism than Key Stage 2 (Preston, 2009). It is worth quoting the following to give the reader an idea of what the government expects of its youth in England:

> Education for citizenship equips young people with the knowledge, skills and understanding to play an effective role in public life. Citizenship encourages them to take an interest in topical and controversial issues and to engage in discussion and debate. Students learn about their rights, responsibilities, duties and freedoms, and about laws, justice and democracy. They learn to take part in decision-making and different forms of action. They play an active role in the life of schools, neighbourhoods, communities and wider society as active and global citizens. Citizenship encourages respect for different national, religious and ethnic identities. It equips students to engage critically with and explore diverse ideas, beliefs, cultures and identities and the values we share as citizens in the UK. Students begin to understand how society has changed and is changing in the UK, Europe and the wider world. (QCDA, 2009b)

The encouragement of engaging with controversial issues in the classroom certainly could stimulate debate about inclusion, cultural diversity and multiculturalism. This makes discussions on debates on 9/11, 7/7 (Eade et al., 2008), the wars in Afghanistan and Iraq, race and racism, faith and multi-faith schooling and different definitions of citizenship possible (Woodman, 2009). The evidence collected for this book within the questionnaires and interviews suggests that some schools are addressing these issues while some schools are not. Taking an interest is very different from increasing understandings and *learning* about difference. Encouraging respect for difference is an important step forward as this means that different identities have to be analysed and the critical, student engagement could theoretically give a national, international and global appreciation of issues concerning individuals and communities within society. Under the heading of Key Skills, at Key Stage 4, comes a sub-heading in the QCDA document entitled 'Identities and Diversity: Living Together in the UK' whereby students should be able to:

A – explore creative approaches to taking action to problems and issues to achieve intended purposes.

B – research, initiate and plan action to address citizenship issues, working individually and with others.

C – negotiate, decide on and take action to try to influence others, bring about change or resist unwanted change.

D – assess critically the impact of their actions on communities and the wider world, now and in the future, and make recommendations to others for further action.

E – reflect on the progress they have made, evaluating what they have learnt from the intended and unintended consequences of action, and the contributions of others as well as themselves. (QCDA, 2009b)

The bullet points above are very general concerning teaching diversity within the concept of citizenship. They are vague in the sense of whose 'problems and issues' are going to be approached. You have to define citizenship issues before you can research and plan action relating to a school curriculum. But what must be remembered is that the above points provide guidance on how to teach and deliver a citizenship curriculum that can be based on issues of diversity and multiculturalism. It is up to the school and practitioner, within the guidance provided by the QCDA (2009a; 2009b) to organize and develop citizenship curricula. However, the issue of resources and the ability to plan citizenship lessons and issues remains the main issue, in both primary and secondary schools, not just within England, concerning whether community actions and contributions can be addressed in schools and the wider community.

In relation to curriculum content, under the heading, 'Range and Content', the study of citizenship at Key Stage 4 should include among the following:

- The impact and consequences of individual and collective actions on communities, including the work of the voluntary sector.
- The origins and implications of diversity and the changing nature of society in the UK, including the perspectives and values that are shared or are common, and the impact of migration and integration on identities, groups and communities.
- The UK role in the world . . . in Europe, the European Union, the Commonwealth and the United Nations. (QCDA, 2009b)

There is real potential in the above list of range of content within citizenship education compared with the vagueness of the previous list concerning Identities and Diversity. Cultural diversity, inclusion and multiculturalism with other contemporary and relevant issues can be included in the curriculum content above. Issues such as anti-discrimination and human rights, democratic processes, *the origins and implications of diversity* (my italics) as well as the role of nation states in the world and the challenges facing the global community are all rich with multicultural possibilities for teaching in the classroom. The issues do not only include what is taught and how it is taught, we need to look at the wider curriculum to see how subjects can be interlinked. There are real possibilities for citizenship combined with Personal, Social and Health Education (PSHE). The subject of PSHE is not new and has been described differently in the past (Best et al., 1995; Best, 2000). A working definition of PSHE is described below by the PSHE Association:

PSHE education is a planned programme of learning opportunities and experiences that help children and young people grow and develop as individuals and as members of families and of social and economic communities. PSHE education supports children and young people to make informed decisions about their lives. It is a planned curriculum area that contributes to pupils' life chances, developing knowledge, understanding, skills and attitudes. (PSHE Association, 2010)

The potential of combining PSHE with citizenship not only allows children and young people of all ages to communicate about personal and social issues, but combined with citizenship, can open up discussions about difference and diversity.

Reflective Exercise

- How can citizenship education focus on both national and international issues?
- How practically in your context can citizenship and PSHE be a good educational subject combination?

The role of teachers and continuing professional development within multicultural education

One of the big issues that came out of respondent data collected for this book was how teachers could improve practice in relation to cultural diversity and multiculturalism. There has been a great deal of evidence published on multicultural education with Banks below highlighting some of the issues relating to multicultural teaching:

> A widely held and disseminated idea in multicultural education is that for it to be effectively implemented within a school, changes must be made in the total school culture as well as within all subject areas, including mathematics and science . . . *Multicultural education is largely a way of viewing reality and a way of thinking, and not just content about various cultures and groups*. Much more important work needs to be done to provide teachers with the examples and specifics they need. In the meantime, we can help all teachers, including mathematics and science teachers, to conceptualize and develop a *equity pedagogy* a way of teaching that is not discipline-specific but has implications for all subject areas and for teaching in general. (Banks, in Lynch et al., 1992: 90–91)

Changing a school culture completely to teach multicultural education is an idea being promoted by Banks and others (e.g. Sleeter and Grant, 2006). And as Banks argues above, this must be in all subjects, not just citizenship and PSHE, because multicultural education is about thinking and viewing reality that concerns *all* cultures and groups. But it's the next line in the Banks (ibid.) quote that needs to be repeated and highlighted: '*. . . work needs to be done to provide teachers with the examples and specifics they need.*' (my italics). That corresponds with what interviewees and those who responded to question-naires were discussing and arguing for in relation to this book. They talked and wrote not only about their education experiences but what was missing in relation to guidance on current issues relating to multicultural education. This is by no means new and as Banks in Lynch et al. (1992) suggests, what was missing was equity pedagogy, meaning teaching and learning which is fair to all students and groups. Ladson-Billings sums up this notion as:

> Inquirers in this field must move beyond an intuitive sense of what is the 'right' kind of teaching for minority students to concrete evidence of peda-gogy and approaches that work. Minority researchers in this area of study are still grappling with questions about what constitutes success . . . If we are going to examine teaching . . . in terms of conception, cognition and context, we must carefully consider the type of pedagogy that is most effective in the minority and / or urban school context. (Ladson-Billings, in Grant, 1992: 115)

Taking examples from the United States (Banks, 2009) forward and focus-ing on teaching 'in terms of conception, cognition and context' we can reflect on a contemporary notion of a multicultural education and pedagogy. A multicultural pedagogy can apply to all groups that is, majority and minorities in all countries. The diversity agenda in England, highlighted by the Ajegbo Report (DfES, 2007) should be applied within education contexts relating to continuing professional development. As Ramsey (2004) suggests, continuing professional development must be supported by schools, communities, local authorities, the state and national governments. Cultural ways of learning (Gutierrez and Rogaff, 2009) are very important in a citizenship curriculum. As Rex suggests:

> One further possibility is that of requiring teachers to take courses in 'racial awareness' in order that they should become aware of and self-critical about they own unconscious beliefs and attitudes. This may have some merit if the teachers concerned see the need for such self-criticism. (Rex, in Sikes and Rizvi, 1997: 116–17)

We need to provide reflective spaces in teaching where practitioners in education can be self-critical about diversity and racism (Gillborn, 2008a; Pollard et al., 2008). Reflective teaching offers the possibility of thinking about an issue like equity pedagogy (Banks, 2009; Bolton, 2010).

As Meier (2002: 179) points out: 'Teachers need spaces to express their feelings and discuss their practice'. This again justifies the call for more continuing professional development for all teachers in education (Collinson et al., 2009; Tang and Choi, 2009). A system of continuing support for practitioners could start at the beginning of a career with teachers being encouraged to reflect on the cultural diversity of different school environments. Schools do work with communities and this is a real part of community cohesion (Cantle, 2008). We are not here talking about parents taking on elements of a teacher's role but the community support and contact that does work relating to children (Stringer et al., 2009). Ramsey (2004) underlines the importance of creating spaces in schools and classrooms for all children to learn, imagine and think with the consequent benefit of increased social and cultural understanding of contemporary issues that concern schools and their communities. And as Cantle suggests, society needs more awareness training . . .

> [which is] . . . generally aimed at employers and decision takers to ensure that they are fully aware of the different needs, customs and practices of other groups, so that they are better able to both avoid inadvertent discrimination and take appropriate positive action measures. This has also included some attempts to persuade people to come to recognise their prejudices, sometimes in very challenging and confrontational sessions, through these techniques are now generally out of favour. Newer style 'diversity training' is much more widely based on all aspects of difference, is less focused on race and consequently has a much more inclusive approach. It is often a former requirement in respect of participation in a number of processes such as recruitment and selection for employment. (Cantle, 2008: 174–78)

By engaging with reflective practice (Bolton, 2010), 'diversity training' will allow all employees and professional practitioners to develop inclusive and multicultural practice through lifelong learning.

The ongoing conceptual debate – Critical Race Theory and interculturalism

The call and desire for more cultural awareness training underlines the need to address and understand racism (Verma, 2007; Cantle, 2008). The concept of anti-racism was raised in Chapter 2 of the book with Troyna (1993) being critical of multiculturalism as a concept for not being dynamic enough to focus on education and racism thereby producing the conditions for social equality and providing greater equal education opportunities. As Race (2009a) acknowledges, Troyna's work is important to revisit not only for raising these issues, but highlighting the need to continue education research in culturally diverse environments. A conceptual idea which develops anti-racist ideas is CRT, which developed from the subject of law in the United States. CRT's aim is to study and transform the relationship between race, racism and power. As Delgardo and Stefancic argue:

> Critical Race Theory . . . not only tries to understand our social situation, but to change it. [CRT] . . . sets out not only to ascertain how society organizes itself along racial lines and hierarchies, but to transform it for the better. (Delgardo and Stefancic, 2001: 2)

CRT theoretically allows people from minority communities to express their voices, feelings and concerns. This has been highlighted in education research (Ladson-Billings, 2004; Gillborn 2008a; 2008b) which has been critical of multicultural conceptual debates.

CRT can provide inclusive opportunities for education research and practice because it questions the power relations that create racism. The education and social policy documents which have been examined in the book have been created with assimilation, integration and multicultural conceptual values in mind. Anti-racism and CRT are important as theoretical concepts because they provide theoretical frameworks for people to be critical of the above concepts and the processes involved in education policy-making to allow an understanding of how difficult it actually is to appreciate the changing nature of cultural diversity in an education classroom. What an examination of anti-racism and CRT also allows is a promotion of racial equality and equity (QCDA, 2009c).

Interculturalism as a concept and intercultural education are further conceptual developments when considering multiculturalism and the teaching of cultural diversity (Alred et al., 2006). Ffye explains that interculturalism provides a space where shared ideas can be discussed in relation to racism and multiculturalism:

> interculturalism stresses both the dynamic nature of cultures and the problematic nature of their interpenetration. If intercultural education provides that necessary common conceptual ground in the field it must be carefully

defined to set it within the broader socio-economic and political context of racism and unequal power relationships. (Ffye, 1993: 46–47)

Shaules provides a very interesting definition of contemporary intercultural learning:

> intercultural learning or cultural learning . . . describe[s] the lived experience of dealing with an unfamiliar cultural environment. This term is intended to include not only the process of immigrants and long-term residents, but also of tourists and short-term visitors. The starting assumption is that both short and long stays in a new cultural environment are learning experiences and involved facing adaptive demands . . . *[a] process of responding to the adaptive demands that result from interacting with a new cultural environment.* (Shaules, 2007: 19–20)

Shaules' notion of adaptation is important here because it highlights the complexity of the lived experience when an individual or community has to deal with difference. Intercultural learning does not only take place in ethe classroom, students are attempting to respond to different and multiple demands within new cultural environments, either travelling abroad or undertaking courses in their home countries but not in their mother tongue. This again makes intercultural teaching and practice, alongside multiculturalism essential as it recognizes the contemporary processes of globalization and the changing nature of cultural diversity (Banks, 2009).

Reflective Exercise

- Is Critical Race Theory a more useful concept to examine cultural diversity than multiculturalism?
- Likewise, is interculturalism more useful as a conceptual tool than multiculturalism?

Summary

It is important to reflect at this stage of the book on several issues which have arisen during this research process on multiculturalism and education. The need to adapt to changing cultural diversity within education is an overall issue and through the process of reflection (Pollard et al., 2008; Bolton, 2010) and comparison of international perspectives (Huat and Kerry, 2008; Banks, 2009) we can increase our understandings of individual and collective practice through continuing professional development.

The first main issue highlights a concern of the dangers of integration as a concept that shapes education policy and practice. By examining the concept of integration alongside social and education policy documents, the issue of a two-way conditional relationship was raised. The policy documents examined, in particular those that created and developed the ideas of 'community cohesion' (HO: 2001) and 'integration and accountability' (HO: 2003) had integration as their conceptual focus. Conditional two-way relationships do not promote community cohesion, cultural diversity, equality or equity. There is also a very thin line between integration and assimilation which is a one-way conditional social relationship with the state controlling the notion of identity. This is enshrined in the metaphor of the 'melting-pot' used in the United States to provide a 'positive' image of immigration in the nineteenth and twentieth centuries. There is nothing multicultural about a 'melting-pot' although other metaphors for example, the 'salad bowl' and the 'mosaic' are starting points to open conceptual debates that still relate to assimilation, integration and multiculturalism in education contexts (Tomlinson, 2008).

The second point to highlight concerns the importance of 'awareness training' (Cantle, 2008) and continuing professional development for practitioners in education. An inclusive, multicultural, anti-racist programme of lifelong learning has to continue to raise social and cultural issues that concern issues, for example racism and discrimination. The citizenship curriculum was examined in this chapter underlining the possibilities of a pluralistic, human rights based curriculum which can raise awareness of multiculturalism within education (Parekh, 2008). Citizenship education has to become statutory in primary schools for children in England and Wales to increase understandings of cultural diversity as early as possible for children (QCDA, 2009a; 2009b). Issues like social segregation and different faith based education need also to be discussed and debated in classrooms (DfES, 2007; DCSF, 2007).

The final point develops the notion of the possibilities of citizenship education which justifies the final chapter on the further conceptual, political and education policy development of citizenship in England. Although Race

(2009b) has argued that the citizenship curriculum in England was originally designed within an integrationist framework, the potential for a multicultural, anti-racist, intercultural curriculum remains (QCDA, 2009b). This is significant when reflecting on Cantle's (2008) notion of community cohesion. This notion was raised by Cremin and Warwick (2008: 47) when they describe it as a '. . . useful vehicle for social, cultural and educational change . . .' but it also has a limited face '. . . of quick fixes and expediency'. Both authors call for a move beyond the 'limited aspects of multiculturalism' which in an English context is useful because citizenship has more educational visibility in the contemporary curriculum to address a variety of culturally diverse issues. But the visibility is clouded when remembering the conceptual underpinning of both integration ideas and the notion of community cohesion. In Chapter 2, it was underlined that English education policy shaped in the 1960s and 1970s (DES, 1967; DES, 1971) was done so within an integrationist conceptual framework. We need to recognize that social and education policy has gone full circle, with policy now being shaped again by integrationist ideas (HO: 2003; DfES, 2004).

The continuing strength of multicultural education does tend to reside outside of England in the United States (Banks, 2009), but the issue of diverse and citizenship based education systems does tend to provide opportunities for culturally diverse education (Banks, 2004). The Ajegbo Report (DfES, 2007) underlined the need to make the National Curriculum in England and Wales more diverse and, as a consequence, allow issues such as focusing on difference, bullying and racism to be researched, debated and discussed in classrooms. What is crucial globally is that diversity and difference not only needs to be examined in all education environments, but understood in relation to society and culture. This idea is highlighted by Cantle:

> In a multicultural country there must be a clear political will to reach a consensus on what level of "difference" is accepted and which differences are acceptable. The practical arrangements also threaten to confound many of the theories, largely because "multiculturalism" does not exist in any meaningful way in many of the communities that make up the so-called multicultural nations, with the same physical separation of minority communities established at the point of initial migration, continuing to a greater or lesser extent thereafter. This has helped to maintain the pretence in the eyes of the majority, that the minorities are separate and distinct, unwilling or unable to develop an affinity to a different culture and simply not part of the same soci-

ety. It may also create a feeling, from the perspective . . . [of minority groups] . . . that they are being denied access to the host society and must cling to their former identities and affinities. (Cantle, 2008: 12–13)

Cantle highlights the dangers of integration and assimilation. Citizenship has to extend the limitations of multiculturalism and move forward an agenda which addresses racism, difference and diversity. Issues such as education and the community and symbolic clothing in schools should be taught by practitioners in most, if not all classrooms and communities (Gereluk, 2006; 2008). Both majority and minority communities have to be reassured that differences can be examined in schools and communities. The dangers and mistrust of issues surrounding a subject as complex as segregation can at the very least be debated and theoretically avoided (Phillips, 2005).

Multiculturalism and education remains contemporary and important as, among many things, it can be an opening for debates concerning cultural diversity, difference, equality, equity and racism. Multiculturalism warns against the two-way and one-way conditional relationships of integration and assimilation policy. Multiculturalism also provides a context for discussion concerning anti-racism, CRT and interculturalism. Multiculturalism as a concept is insightful when examining the conceptual link between citizenship, integration and education policy. And that is the aim of the final chapter when we attempt to examine the conceptual move in England from a more multicultural citizenship to integrationist citizenship.

Useful websites

Citizenship Foundation
   www.citizenshipfoundation.org.uk/main/page.php?286
Curriculum Review – Diversity and Citizenship. The Ajegbo Report (DfES, 2007)
   publications.teachernet.gov.uk/eOrderingDownload/DfESDiversity&Citizenship.pdf
Department of Education (DfE)
   www.education.gov.uk/
Education Guardian
   www.guardian.co.uk/education
The Independent Education
   www.independent.co.uk/news/education/
National Foundation for Educational Research – Citizenship and Human Rights Education
   www.nfer.ac.uk/research-areas/citizenship/

PSHE Association

www.pshe-association.org.uk/secondary_curriculum.aspx

Qualifications and Curriculum Development Agency

www.qcda.gov.uk/

Teaching and Development Agency for Schools

www.tda.gov.uk/

Times Higher Education Supplement

www.timeshighereducation.co.uk/

From Multicultural Citizenship to Integrationist Citizenship

Introduction

In relation to multiculturalism and the consequences for education, an extremely significant conceptual movement, has been the ideological shift from multicultural to integrationist citizenship (Race, 2012; 2014). Will Kymlicka (1995; 2007; 2012) is known as a key advocate of multicultural citizenship within both a Canadian and more global context. As Crowder (2013: 38) argues, Kymlicka is important because, '. . . he constructs a direct link between multiculturalism and liberal democracy, the political system in which multiculturalist principles and policies have in fact emerged in the last forty years.' It is that link between multiculturalism and politics, as well as Kymlicka highlighting the issues concerning national minorities and ethnic differences which is socially important as it highlights the role of state policy-making in both multicultural and integrationist contexts. Kymlicka's work will shortly be examined to increase understandings of multicultural citizenship but also the changing context of this conceptual shift towards intergrationist policy. Bikhu Parekh (2000) and James Banks' (2014) work will then be examined to highlight the continued need for a multicultural rather than a monocultural education. Changes in citizenship caused by integrationist terms and policy (Joppke, 2010; 2012) have led to a political debate which surrounds on the one hand a more multicultural European citizenship, and on the other hand a more national integration policy defined by Joppke as civic integration. That political debate will be further analysed by examining political speeches made by Angela Merkel, David Cameron and Nick Clegg in relation to both multiculturalism and integration. The developments concerning citizenship curriculum in England will then be highlighted by examining first the Equality Act of 2010, followed by the Education Act (DfE, 2011) which witnessed a political change of direction for citizenship towards a more integrationist inspired curricula in England at Key Stage 3 and 4 that is secondary school students aged between 11 and 16 (Race, 2012). The chapter will end with a summary concerning this movement from multiculturalism to integrationist citizenship (Race, 2014) and the consequences this has for education in both English and international contexts.

Kymlicka and multicultural citizenship

Multiculturalism, for Kymlicka (2012: 8) was '. . . first and foremost about developing new models of democratic citizenship, grounded in human rights ideas, to replace earlier uncivil and undemocratic relations of hierarchy and exclusion . . .' Multiculturalism was about constructing new and relevant civic and political relations to overcome social and cultural inequalities. This was important because Kymlicka (1995: 11) recognized that cultural diversity within a state involved the coexistence of different ethnicities and therefore different diverse cultures which involved many national minorities rather than one nation. Therefore, '. . ."nation" means a historical community, more or less institutionally complete, occupying a given territory or homeland, sharing a distinct language and culture. A "nation" in this sociological sense is closely related to the idea of a "people" or a "culture" – indeed, these concepts are often defined in terms of each other.' Kymlicka (1995) sets out the notion of a multi-nation which encompasses cultural diversity. As Crowder (2013: 7) suggests when defining multiculturalism, '. . . the multiplicity of cultures within a single society should be not only generally approved of but also given positive recognition in the public policy and public institutions of the society.' So it is important to go beyond simple recognition and tolerance of difference to social and cultural approval of peoples (Stepan and Taylor, 2014). In many respects, we have to move beyond our own culture or as Crowder (2013) implies, the culture we have grown up in to at the very least increase our understandings of difference. Crowder (2013: 47) also suggests that '. . . people do not change their cultural affiliations readily . . . people tend to remain within the culture that formed them.' Some people do change cultural affiliations but this is a difficult process. When considering this change, Kymlicka is underlining, as Crowder (ibid.) implies, '. . . that equal treatment might require special compensation for minority cultural groups and that cultural membership . . . of one's culture, is essential to individual freedom'. The social and cultural approval of peoples by the modern state and majority population focuses towards ongoing political debates which surround immigration.

The term immigration has always been political and has been used to promote political interests rather than acknowledging the cultural, social, economic, as well as educational influences of minority groups (Race, 2014). New and relevant civic and political relations have always involved immigration within the nation state. Within a multicultural framework, cultural pluralism is essential and a nation exhibits this if

> . . . it accepts large numbers of individuals and families from other cultures as immigrants, and allows them to maintain some of their ethic particularity . . . Immigrant groups are not 'nations', and do not occupy homelands. Their distinctiveness is manifested primarily in their family lives and in voluntary associations, and is not inconsistent with their institutional integration . . . The commitment to ensuing a common language has been a constant feature of the history of immigration policy. (Kymlicka, 1995: 13–14)

What, I would suggest, needs to be continually analysed is how far the state intervenes in relation to the individual and family lives and how the boundaries of cultural pluralism were affected by integrationist policy. The danger in Kymicka's (2012: 15) eyes was '. . . the proliferation of "civic integration" policies, typically in the form of obligatory language and county knowledge requirements' (Joppke, 2012). 'Requirements of civic integration in different countries was the citizenship test and the possession of Identification cards.' These civic integration policies represent as Lyon (2009) argues, a phase in the long term attempts of states to find stable ways of identifying citizens. What should remain within the idea of multiculturalism-as-citizenization, as Kymlicka (2012) suggests is the multiculturalism–integration debate and the obstacles that prevent new modules of multicultural citizenship should be at the very least debated.

In this sense, Kymlicka's work (1995; 2007; 2012) on multiculturalism is important because its focus is not only on the national and international citizen but on national and ethnic differences. Kymlicka's intention was to always look at multiculturalism which arose from national and ethnic differences. 'National' minorities include indigenous peoples and regional groups like the Basques and Catalans in Spain. As Crowder (2013: 49) underlines, 'By contrast, "ethnic" minorities are immigrant groups whose members have chosen to become part of a new society. In doing so, they usually bring their beliefs and values with them, embedded in "their language and historical narratives", but they tacitly agree to leave behind the institutions and social practices which this vocabulary originally referred to and made sense of.' It is that tacit agreement which is most interesting and has a lot of consequences for all members of ethnic minority groups. It almost reverses Williams' (2013) idea of the multicultural dilemma with the state having to react to new immigrants and ethnic minorities. Moreover, the tacit agreement involves the individual and how s/he reacts to social and cultural choices. Furthermore, the tacit agreement is shaped by the nation state through policy-making. As Crowder (2013: 50) suggests, assimilation implies a total tacit agreement between the individual / group towards the state. Integration allows for more flexibility: 'Nevertheless, the acceptability of integration in the case of ethnic minorities contrasts strongly with the entitlement of national minorities to lead, in some substantial sense, an independent existence.' And where does multiculturalism or multiculture in for example, a British context (Pathak, 2008) fit into this equation?

As Kymlicka (1995: 18) underlines, he uses, '... a "culture" as synonymous with "a nation" or "a people" – that is, as in intergenerational community, more or less institutionally complete, occupying a given territory or homeland, sharing a distinct language and history.' The state is multicultural if its national minorities are distinct and self-governing societies which are merged into the larger state are distinct from ethnic groups who are immigrants who have left their nation to enter another nation. For some people as Kymlicka (1995:

23–24) argues, '. . . national membership should be based solely on accepting political principles of democracy and rights, rather than integration into a particular culture.' So Kymlicka defines what he means by multiculturalism here and makes the crucial distinction between multiculturalism which is defined by national minorities and ethnic groups and integration which is not defined here in his work.

Kymlicka (2007: 8) highlights the complexities of internationalizing multiculturalism arguing that, '. . . political manipulation of state-minority relations [has] the danger of reverting back to more illiberal and undemocratic relations concerning national minorities and ethnic groups'. As Kymlicka (2007: 296–98) suggests, increasing democratic citizenship must be an international rather than a domestic project which would involve active participation by all citizens in both majority and minority communities. But this idea in itself raises major dilemmas with the collaboration of nation states, as well as non-state actors from different regions of the world. Is a multicultural citizenship possible within a global world in the twenty-first century? In partial answer to that question, multicultural citizenship is politically controlled through policy which has consequences for individual rights. Kymlicka's theories are also about rights and the control of cultural rights because cultural membership of a state involves individual and group choice and who has the right to choose in relation to assimilation, integration and multicultural existences. Some citizens have more choices or the right to choose and when thinking of Bourdieu's (2005; 2010; Bourdieu and Passeron, 1990) theoretical ideas, these citizens have more cultural capital than others to make social choices for example the option of choosing home education rather than sending children to school (Ball, 2003; Race, 2014). It is that control through policy of cultural and social choices that we will examine later in the chapter when we examine recent political speeches which concern multicultural and integrationist policies and their consequences for national or international citizenship.

Reflective Exercise

- What is more important – the national or international citizen? Why is one more important than the other?
- To what extent is multicultural citizenship possible within a global world?

Parekh and Banks – the continued need for multicultural education

Within a book examining Multiculturalism and Education, it is significant to apply Kymlicka's work on multicultural citizenship and his ideas based on the distinction between national minority, ethnic difference and the need to move beyond recognition and tolerance to approval when considering cultural rights to a multicultural education that can begin to promote and advocate the need for this continuing debate and advancing a curricula based on multicultural citizenship (Race, 2012; 2014). This is why we return and reflect upon Bikhu Parekh's (2000; 2008) and James Banks' (2007; 2014) work as we did in Chapter 2 of this book. Parekh (2000: 225–26) is a supporter of multicultural over monocultural education. The limitations of monocultural curricula are obvious for Parekh with students' 'intellectual curiosity' being dulled with students' perspectives of their own cultures being narrowed, let alone having the opportunity to study cultural difference. Parekh (2000: 226–27) also claims, 'Monocultural education also tends to breed arrogance, insensitivity and racism . . . Monocultural education, then, is simply not good education.' Multicultural education is more inclusively focused education and the principle of multicultural education has to be expressed through a multicultural curriculum which subsequently allows multicultural citizenship to be taught, critiqued and developed. For Harty and Marty (2005: 102) multicultural citizenship consists of, '. . . democracy, equality, recognition, identity [and] trust . . .', with the authors recognizing that some of the dimensions might matter more than others as well as implying that multicultural citizenship is highly political. If as Parekh (2000: 230) claims, '. . . multicultural education is an education in freedom, both in the sense of freedom *from* ethnocentric prejudices and biases and freedom *to* explore and learn from other cultures and perspectives . . .', the issue then becomes how can multicultural citizenship be taught within multicultural education.

Banks (2007), from within an American perspective, gives us insights into how multicultural education can be developed and not only for multicultural citizenship inspired curricula within education. He highlights the need to change education to make it more contemporary and relevant to students and teachers. Education, as Banks (2007: 13) argues, needs to be able to help all students, '. . . to acquire the knowledge, attitudes, and skills need to function effectively in today's knowledge society. Our schools were designed for a different population at a time when immigrant and low-income youths did not need to be literate or to have basic skills to get jobs and to become self-supporting citizens'. For Banks, multicultural education is:

- *an idea or concept, and*
- [an] *educational reform movement and*
- *a process.* (Banks, 2014: 1)

Multicultural education means that all students should have equal opportunities to learn in school. As Banks (ibid.) continues: 'Multicultural education . . . also assumes that diversity enriches a nation and increases the ways in which its citizens can perceive and solve personal and public problems.' Banks (2014: 7) implies that education needs to change for a more multicultural focus, and an effective citizenship education can help students '. . . to acquire the knowledge skills, and values needed to function effectively within their cultural communities, nation-states, regions, and the global community.' The concept of multicultural education then needs to focus on a more culturally diverse and citizenship-orientated curriculum. Multicultural education then can theoretically shape curriculum delivery and for these changes to take place, in Banks' words, an educational reform movement is needed to instigate this change both in the United States and around the world. Banks (2014: 23), similarly to Parekh and Kymlicka, all recognize that this will not be easy as 'We are living in a dangerous, confused, and troubled world that demands leaders, educators, and classroom teachers who can bridge cultural, ethnic, and religious borders, envision new possibilities, invent novel *paradigms*, and engage in personal transformation and visionary action.'

Reflective Exercise

- How can multicultural citizenship be taught in multicultural education?
- What are the knowledge, skills and values needed to function effectively within the global community?

Joppke – European citizenship and civic integration

The educational changes that Banks calls for are indeed very difficult when we compare integrationist with multiculturalist citizenship. As Christian Joppke (2010) argues, evolving citizenship presents a paradox with huge and growing disparities of wealth and security on the one hand, but people being connected more than ever on the other hand by technology and ideas. That connection should bring people together in both common and global citizenship. However, the inequity and inequality will divide citizens along intersectional lines (Bhopal and Preston, 2012). Joppke (2010: 156) also raises the political issue of immigration with, '. . . the function of citizenship talk is to be found less in its illocutionary purpose of integrating newcomers than in its perlocutionary effect of pacifying ill-disposed natives.' Joppke calls for the future of citizenship to be based on a European Union (EU) citizenship, free from the ideals of nationhood and nationalism and a national citizenship. But political realities as we will show with the political speeches of Merkel, Cameron and Clegg later in this chapter provide a somewhat different political reality to Joppke's ideas. Despite this, Joppke argues:

> In reality, the court-driven empowerment of European citizenship casts a long shadow over contemporary state campaigns to upgrade the worth of national citizenship. If the British state seeks to attach more rights to the status of citizenship and in parallel to lessen the attractions of the legal permanent residence alternative, this is entirely futile: European Union law commands the inclusion of all EU foreigners and of long-settled immigrants into any upgraded national citizen privileges. (Joppke, 2010: 171–72)

So we have a political clash between European citizenship based on a multicultural model that encourages inclusion and economic movement based on European law and the more integrationist citizenship based on the preservation of the nation state. Joppke (2012) examines the policy of 'civic integration' in the Netherlands in the late 1990s where the policy was to integrate immigrants from Turkish and Moroccan communities into host- society institutions, above all the labour market. The aim was not only to make the immigrant learn Dutch but to facilitate access to employment. As Joppke (2012: 2) underlines: 'The goal was to make them [the immigrant] learn Dutch, not as a matter of "national identity" but to facilitate better access to employment.

The objective was to make the immigrant in this case study, Dutch. Due to growing populism and domestic turmoil surrounding Muslims and Islam . . . an initially neoliberal policy of making immigrants "self-sufficient" (and thus no longer dependent on welfare) morphed into a culture-focused policy of making them adapt to, or at least be cognizant of, "Dutch norms and values". Residence permits in the Netherlands at this time, were contingent upon the immigrant passing a civic integration exam which was extended to temporary visas where migrants had to show this knowledge before arrival (the so-called integration from abroad) test (ibid.). Joppke's example shows how civic integration in the Netherlands was quickly extended to nationality law through a citizenship test.

Merry (2013: 21) raises an interesting argument when looking at integration and citizenship: 'If integration is for equality and for citizenship then a democratic society will function more effectively when persons or groups are not segregated from one another but interact across their respective differences.' If this to be achieved when reflecting on civic integration or 'integration from abroad' (Joppke, 2012) then there should be a more multicultural approach when considering ethnic differences and national minorities (Kymlicka, 2012) with immigrant communities are acknowledged and celebrated. Merry suggests that mixed neighbourhoods with different communities and school environments are the cultural arenas which can ensure good citizenship. Merry (2013: 32) argues: 'Schools are very often the focal point of these discussions because they arguably present the best chance for children from different backgrounds to cross these seemingly naturally occurring divides.' Merry goes on to define good citizenship through the following terms:

- Tolerance
- Social Trust
- Mutual Cooperation. (Merry, 2013: 33)

Merry (2013) is critical of the notion of good citizenship because of the limited duration of interactions between communities and the significance of contact in cultural and educational environments. The integration-for-citizenship argument not only eludes reality but the state as Joppke (2012) underlines in his Dutch example, can have tremendous influence through general state policies for example school curricula and more specific policies of civic integration and the more national tendencies of an 'integration from abroad' policy. For Merry (2013: 60), citizenship theory, '. . . arguably consists of shared membership in a political space on the basis of mutual moral and legal rights and responsibilities broadly understood.' As Race (2011; 2014) argues, mutual shared membership is conditioned and influenced by the state and rights and responsibilities are terms used in many education policy documents to influence the choices individuals and groups have when making cultural and social decisions. And as Merry (2013: 62) acknowledges, when thinking of the conception of citizenship, either integrationist or multicultural, the state has to reconcile its aims with the diverse array of beliefs and practices among society's members which is the biggest ongoing cultural challenge that all nation states face (Joppke, 2012).

Reflective Exercise

- What is the purpose of the citizenship test?
- How would you define good citizenship?
- How does a nation state reconcile its aims through policy with the diverse array of belief and practices among its society's members?

Modood is correct on his views concerning integration when he suggests that:

> . . . all attempted models of integration, not just in Britain but across Europe, are in crisis. We can however have a better sense of what the issues are and so what needs to be done if, firstly, we recognise that discourses of integration and multiculturalism are exercises in conceptualising post-immigration difference and as such operate at three distinct levels: as an (implicit) sociology; as a political response; and as a vision of what is the whole in which difference is to be integrated. Depending upon the sociology in question certain political responses are possible or not, more reasonable or less. The sociological and political assumptions are thus mutually dependent. (Modood, 2011: 75)

It is important to understand that these opening sections of this chapter underline the need when examining multicultural and integrationist citizenship that this is a conceptual exercise to increase our understandings of what is happening in cultural, social, economic and political arenas. This is not exclusively a political issue that universally concerns immigration and the consequent political response. This analysis has also to be sociological to understand the wider cultural complexity when examining ethnic difference or national minorities (Kymlicka, 2012). The mutual dependency goes beyond political and sociological assumptions and has to when examining cultural diversity, race and ethnicity (Race and Lander, 2014). As Callan (2007: 175) argues, '... the reasonable citizen is disposed to propose fair terms of cooperation to others, to settle differences in mutually acceptable ways, and to abide by agreed terms of cooperation so long as others are prepared to do likewise.' But as Pattie et al. (2004) argue, citizens are more willing to cooperate if they face relative equality that ensures that more people can face common problems together. If there is greater social and cultural inequity and division then creating a 'good citizenship' (Merry, 2013) seems to become a harder task. As Modood (2011) acknowledges above, when increasing our understandings of integrationist and multicultural discourses, we have to examine the political responses to this debate and in the next section we will examine English and international responses to multiculturalism which have implications for both integration and citizenship.

Is multiculturalism dead? – Part 2 – Merkel, Cameron and Clegg

Multiculturalism and Education is fundamentally shaped by politics and is inherently political. This section looks at the wider political debates which has shaped multiculturalism not only in England but abroad. In this section, there are three political speeches, delivered between October 2010 and March 2011 which are worth examining in relation to the perceived and repeated 'Death of Multiculturalism' discourse examined in Chapter 3 of this book. The first was given by the German Chancellor, Angela Merkel in Potsdam, Germany in October 2010. The second speech, which was the one commented on most frequently by the English-speaking media, was The Prime Minister of the United Kingdom (UK) David Cameron's speech in Munich in February 2011 (Mahamdallie, 2011). The final speech was given by Nick Clegg, the Deputy Prime Minister of the United Kingdom in Luton in March 2011. These speeches are worthy of examination in detail because of their political contexts, how they were reported and what consequences they had for multiculturalism in Europe and beyond.

Reflective Exercise

- How political is multiculturalism and education?
- How can a politician shape policy and political opinion?

The first thing to note when considering Angela Merkel's speech about multicultural Germany was her political perspective and position as she gave her speech in front of younger members of the Christian Democratic Union Party (CDU). In this sense, an issue of balance has to be considered in relation to the tone of the speech. Merkel (BBC, 2010) stated: 'the approach [to build] a multicultural [society] and to live side-by-side and to enjoy each other . . . has failed, utterly failed.' However, in her speech, Merkel also made it clear that immigrants were also welcome in Germany. The second issue was how the speech was translated and reported in the English media. As Piller (2010) argues: 'The headline "multiculturalism has failed" is an incorrect translation of "Multikulti ist absolut gescheitert" because "MultiKulti" is not "multiculturalism". Germany has never had a policy of multiculturalism and the idea continues to be that migrants integrate into a dominant German culture.' So, Piller (2010) touches on the German history of integration rather than multiculturalism. As Lanz (2010) argues, the history of Germany, as well as its immigration policy has to be recognized to understand the perceived German model of multiculturalism. Reunification of Germany took place in 1991, and Berlin is perhaps the best example of the complexity of Germany having been divided into East and West after the Second World War. Ironically as Lanz (2001: 104) highlights, Berlin was the first West German state to pursue its own multicultural integration policy. Post-1991 immigration issues have been visible in German politics, none more so than the issues concerning Turkish immigration.

Indeed, before Merkel's speech in October 2010, Germany held talks with Turkey, in which both countries pledged to improve the often poor integration record of Germany's estimated 2.5 million Turkish community (BBC, 2010). The main issue that affected the Turkish-origin migrant population in German was the principal of the German state disallowing multiple citizenship. As Zapata-Barrero and Gropas (2012: 175) highlight, thousands of people with Turkish descent applied for reapproval of their Turkish passports after being naturalized into the German state in early 2000. As a consequence, they had their German citizenship withdrawn and also lost their permanent residence status, for which they were forced to reapply. As Zapata-Barrero and Gropas,

(2012) continue, the German state had denied double citizenship to Turkish migrants who felt they were being targeted. Merkel in her speech therefore had to strike a political balance, 'pandering to her party's conservative sensibilities . . .' but moreover as Piller (2010) underlines, saying that 'multikulti has completely failed' but furthermore accepting diversity and particularly Muslims as a legitimate part of the imagined German nation. It was not just her political party or the Turkish immigrant population that Merkel was addressing in her speech (Tournon, 2013). Wasmer (2013: 16) sums up the ambiguity of German multiculturalism: 'Germany has never stood as the prototype of a multicultural society and it does not do so now . . . but Germany has adopted more multicultural policies.' As Wasmer continues:

> Although current usage of 'multicultural' of *multikulti* signals the problems that Germany's multiculturalism is faced with, the term is seldom used explicitly at the centre of public debates over relevant issues. Three key areas of debate can be identified (although they are closely interwoven): (1) Immigration to Germany; (2) the multicultural reality in Germany – perceptions and assessments of positive and, mostly, negative aspects of ethnic diversity; and (3) ideas about how to deal with a multicultural reality. (Wasmer, 2013: 170)

Merkel's speech was followed in February 2011 by the UK Prime Minister, David Cameron who was talking at a security conference in Munich (Mahamdallie, 2011). Cameron talked about state multiculturalism but his tone and direction were different to Merkel. Cameron (2011) talked about multiculturalism and segregation: 'Under the doctrine of state multiculturalism, we have encouraged different cultures to live separate lives, apart from each other and apart from the mainstream. We've failed to provide a vision of society to which they want to belong. We've even tolerated these segregated communities behaving in ways that run completely counter to our values.' The issue of difference is raised here and cultures leading separate lives when the key aim of multiculturalism is to celebrate cultural diversity rather than focusing on 'our values'. The notion of integration is highlighted when Cameron (2011) mentions '. . . people "liv[ing] apart when we need a clear sense of shared national identity . . ."' rather than living together within a culturally diverse society. This seems to encourage more integration and separation rather than celebrating difference.

Another theme that Cameron (2011) touches upon is the concept of citizen. The Prime Minister calls for 'less passive tolerance . . . and a much more muscular liberalism. The term muscular liberalism is left undefined' but Cameron who '. . . believes in certain values [and a country] that actively promotes them.' Certain values, also remain undefined, but if we 'actively promote' these values: It says to its citizens, this is what defines us as a society: to belong here is to believe in these things (Cameron, 2011). One of these values includes, '. . . making sure that immigrants speak the language of their new home and ensuring that people are educated in the elements of a common culture and curriculum.' I would suggest that this is another integrationist example of supporting a national or 'common' curriculum rather than a culturally diverse-based curriculum that educates and celebrates diversity rather than trying to eliminate cultural difference. The CfBT / British Council (2014) also highlight the complexity of language teaching in English schools. The significant issues raised through the 2013/2014 survey in the report are:

- The need for further training of primary school teachers
- The lack of cohesion at the transition from Key Stage 2 to Key Stage 3
- The growing exclusion of certain groups of pupils from language study at Key Stages 3 and 4
- The deep crisis of language study post-16. (CfBT / British Council, 2014: 9)

So modern foreign language (MFL) teaching itself needs addressing through continuing professional development of teachers in nursery and primary schools as well as a focus on language study and teacher training post-16. Which schools can teach MFL and what resources are required needs to be continuously debated. Cameron (2011) focuses again on citizenship when he discusses a 'National Citizen Service' with a theoretical 2-month scheme for 16-year-olds from different backgrounds to live and work together. This seems to be another movement towards a national citizen(ship) and when Cameron talks about 'active participation' with 'the balance of power [moving] away from the state towards to people', the Prime Minister is ultimately attempting to focus on national identity (singular) rather than cultural identities 'plural'. When Cameron (2011) talks about '. . . a much broader and generous vision of citizenship . . .' it is in fact, not a broad vision, but a more structured, political and conditional notion of citizenship that is an integrationist rather than a multicultural citizenship.

Reflective Exercise

- How affective were the political speeches of Merkel and Cameron?
- How important is language teaching within a national curriculum? Which languages should be taught in schools and why?
- How would a 'national citizen service' work?

Nick Clegg in March 2011, responded to David Cameron's speech, and focuses more on multiculturalism. The title of his speech does tend to suggest he is elaborating and developing some of Cameron's (2011) ideas but the inclusion of 'multicultural society' indicates that the idea of multiculturalism remains very much alive. Indeed, with Merkel (BBC, 2010) and Cameron (2011) both engaging with the idea, Clegg (2011) broadens its political application and clarifies the confused media and political link between Islam and Terrorism by defining who the extremists are in the United Kingdom: '. . . There are nationalistic or racist extremists, like the members of the English Defence League, or the British National Party. There are black extremists like the Nation of Islam, There are Muslim extremists like the members of Islam 4 UK.' This is something Cameron (2011) failed to do in his speech in Munich. Clegg (2011) also discusses individual rights and responsibilities. As has already been highlighted in this book in Chapter 2, 'responsibilities' is a term that has been used in education policy documentation since the 1960s. Clegg (2011) mentions: '. . . the rights and responsibilities of individual identity makes it even more important to balance individual liberty and collective responsibility . . .' but the issues remain the same, whose responsibilities – the state or the individual? And Clegg (2011) provides the answer: 'But we are clear that individuals need to take responsibility . . .'. The individual remains responsible for his / her behaviour and that is a condition continually highlighted within law and through education policy. The issue here concerns how an individual or group responds to that responsibility.

Clegg (2011) cites Bhikhu Parekh in his speech when he underlines that we are '. . . a community of citizens and a community of communities'. It is worth looking at Parekh's (2000; 2008; 2011) comments on citizens and communities to increase understandings of what Clegg (2011) was attempting to develop here. Parekh (2000) wrote that multicultural society. '. . . sees itself both as a community of citizens and a community of communities, *and hence as a community of communally embedded and attached individuals* (my emphasis)'. Parekh argues that community embeddedment is crucial for everyone and communities are open and interactive rather than threatened or frozen. Parekh calls for more inclusive rather than exclusive communities. Individuals can be attached to a community and communities are continuingly changing and evolving identities can nurture '. . . a community of communities based on the kind of plural collective culture . . .' (Parekh, 2000: 340–41). The notion of change is important here as cultures not only change but evolve and as Merry (2013) underlines, the nation state has to attempt to keep up with these social and cultural changes. Clegg (2011) develops the idea of muscular liberalism which is based around and is integral to the 'culture of dialogue' (Parekh, 2000: 340) whereby '. . . Muscular liberals flex their muscles in open argument . . . If we are truly confident about the strength of our liberal values we should be confident about their ability to defeat the inferior arguments of our opponents'. Dialogue needs to be the starting point when acknowledging cultural diversity alongside its evolving and changing nature.

Clegg (2011) then considers the meaning and issue of multiculturalism: 'For me, multiculturalism has to [be] seen as a process by which people respect and communicate with each other, rather than build walls between each other. Welcoming diversity but resisting division: that's the kind of multiculturalism of an open, confident society.' The first issue here is the perceived focus on intersectional diversity over division. The focus has to emcompass all diversity and not exclusively cultural. As Clegg (2011) continues: 'And the cultures in a multicultural society are not just ethnic or religious. Many of the cultural issues of the day cut right across these boundaries: gay rights; the role of women; identities across national borders; differing attitudes to marriage . . .' The lack of any intersectional engagement is clear in all three of the speeches examined in this section. The second issue is that the debate over cultural disagreements that Merkel (BBC, 2010), Cameron (2011) and Clegg (2011) are talking about are much more complex than much of the debate implies. Clegg (2011) theoretically moves away from liberal beliefs when he argues: 'Maintaining a liberal, open nation also demands a fierce allegiance to shared values. The values of liberal citizenship. The values of responsibility, tolerance and openness.' And it is the 'shared values' rather than the culturally diverse values which are being recognized here. Openness is conditionally set out within the nation state for example the National Curriculum which is integrationist not multiculturalist in nature (Race, 2012). What is being implied here is that liberal citizenship is political and integrationist rather than multicultural. Parekh underlines the complexity of defining a multicultural society:

> A multicultural society is characterized by cultural diversity. Multiculturalism represents a particular approach to that diversity and is a normative doctrine. In my *Rethinking Multiculturalism*, [2000] I examine the concept of multicultural society and show what kind and degree of diversity a society should display in order to be called multicultural. After all, all societies display some diversity, and to call them all multicultural is to deprive the concept of coherence and meaning. (Parekh, 2011: 65)

Some societies are therefore more multicultural than others meaning culturally diversity has to continually be promoted everywhere. There are differences to how both Cameron (2011) negatively and Clegg (2011) more positively define multiculturalism (Latour, 2012). It is also worth highlighting how both Merkel (BBC, 2010) and Clegg (2011) are also similar in at the very least acknowledging cultural difference and its importance in both German and English society. Furthermore, Clegg (2011) moves from liberalism to Coalition politics when he talks about 'a fierce allegiance to liberal citizenship' which seems more integrationist that is 'the fierce national allegiance' which is more integrationist than multicultural. As Parekh (2010: 341) argues, a multicultural society, '... cherishes not static and ghettoized, but interactive and dynamic, multiculturalism'. However, as Merry (2013) argued above, it is how a state reacts to cultural diversity and difference within policy which shapes policy and whether, as we will see in the sections below, a subject like citizenship is either integrationist or multicultural (Race, 2014).

Reflective Exercise

- How can nation states be 'a community of citizens and a community of communities'?
- To what extent is Clegg's speech more multicultural than integrationist?

The Equality Act (2010) and The Education Act (DfE, 2011)

The reason why both the Equality Act and The Education Act (DfE, 2011) legislation are being analysed here is the connections they both have with the school curriculum and specifically curriculum content in England. The Equality Act of 2010 replaced legislation and regulations and provided a single, consolidated source of discrimination law. It became unlawful for a school to discriminate against a pupil or prospective pupil by treating them less favourably because of their:

- sex,
- race,
- disability,

- religion or belief,
- sexual orientation,
- gender reassignment, pregnancy or maternity. (DfE, 2013: 5)

In terms of curriculum, the **content** (in bold within the document) of the school curriculum has never been prosecuted by anyone concerning discrimination law and the Equality Act (2010) now states that curriculum content is excluded from the legislation. However, the way in which a school provides education – the **delivery** (in bold within the document) of the curriculum – is explicitly included in the legislation (DfE, 2013a: 12). This comment and consequence of the Equality Act legislation has major impact for education. Delivery issues range from teaching of professional practitioners to the learning of students in relation to the delivery of curriculum. The importance of delivery over content is now also pronounced within education through the Equality Act (2010) legislation. Teachers and lecturers now have to be more considerate in relation to anti-discrimination legislation. Moreover, practitioners have to reflect on how curriculum content is delivered in the classroom and lecture theatre. As the DfE (ibid.) highlights: 'Excluding the content of the curriculum ensures that schools are free to include a full range of issues, ideas and materials in their syllabus, and to expose pupils to thoughts and ideas of all kinds, however challenging and controversial . . . But schools will need to ensure that the way in which issues are taught does not subject individual pupils to discrimination.' It is also interesting at how contradictory the issue of content and delivery is in relation to education and specifically the citizenship curriculum which will shortly be examined in detail within this chapter by looking at the content guidelines of Key Stage Four (DfE, 2013c). This issue relates to delivery and how a citizenship curriculum be taught by both primary and secondary teachers, as well as in further and higher education when only secondary school teachers are qualified specifically in the subject of citizenship.

One of the more important but less examined consequences of the Education Act (DfE, 2011) was the abolition of the Qualification and Curriculum Development Agency (QCDA). In the Education Act (DfE, 2011) hidden away on page 95 of the legislative document is a mention of OfQual (2014) which was created to deal with regulating qualifications within the national curriculum. OfQual claim independence but give advice to Government and specifically to the Department for Education on qualifications and assessment. The curriculum, let alone curriculum content, is not mentioned and is not part of OfQual's remit. Qualification regulation at Key Stages 1–4 is now under OfQual guidance while curriculum decisions, choices and changes are now focused within the DfE. Having looked in the previous chapter of this book at the QCDA, I want to now compare the potential of citizenship curriculum (QCDA, 2009) with the citizenship curriculum of Key Stage 4 at the DfE (2013b; 2013c).

Reflective Exercise

- How does a school apply discriminatory law in relation to the above six bullet points (DfE, 2013)?
- In terms of school curriculum, is content more important than delivery?
- Should equal opportunities be at the centre of education curriculum?

Disapplying the Citizenship Curriculum in England at Key Stages 3 and 4

When we consider curriculum content and delivery, we have to examine education policy-making and see how politics influences and shapes how the curriculum is made and changes. This section shows how citizenship curriculum has changed since the Coalition government came into power in 2010. The Department for Education in '. . . July 2012 listed 4,238 publications related to education and cognate matters . . .' (Ball, 2013: 2) on its website, which was consequently closed in 2013 with educational information for all key and foundations subjects taught in schools in England being moved to Gov.Uk. There is also an interesting issue in relation to the Citizenship Programmes of Study which were on the DfE website in 2013 but have now been placed in the UK Government Web Archive which is now virtually accessible, or harder to access, in the National Archive (DfE, 2013c). What is clear is that citizenship curricula and information on how to teach in schools is harder to find in 2014 than it was in 2009. This became the case after the QCDA was closed (DfE, 2011) with information moving to the DfE's own website before moving again to Gov.Uk. Significantly, citizenship lost its statutory status as a foundation subject in September 2013 at Key Stages 3 and 4 in England

and as the DfE (2013c) underline, '... schools are free to develop their own curricula for citizenship that best meets the needs of their pupils ...' for the new national curriculum starting in September 2014. What is important to highlight here is the potential of citizenship education for professional practice to teach more cultural diversity has diminished as information first on Programmes of Study and curricula options for citizenship become harder to find. The evidence which is available on the National Archive website is a three-page document on Citizenship Programmes of Study (DfE, 2013b) at Key Stages 3 and 4 which applies to a more detailed document on Citizenship Key Stage 4 (DfE, 2013c) content on Programmes of Study and Attainment Target Level Descriptors.

When examining the document on Citizenship Programmes of Study, Key Stage 4 Citizenship teaching should, '... deepen pupils' understanding of democracy, government and the rights and responsibilities of citizens ...'. Pupils should be taught about:

> parliamentary democracy and the key elements of the constitution of the United Kingdom, including the power of government, the role of citizens and Parliament. (DfE, 2013b: 2)

It is significant to pause here and underline that most nation states have a written constitution unlike the United Kingdom who has an unwritten constitution. The constitution sets out the highest laws of each country. Highest laws are written down and codified in most countries. The highest laws are not written down in one single document in the United Kingdom. Common Law is found in court decisions (Judiciary) and Parliamentary legislation (the legislature). Hopefully, the above information is explained to students at Key Stage 3 before the political complexity of Common Law is explained alongside UK devolution post-1997 which involves both a Welsh and Northern Ireland Assembly and a Scottish Parliament, which could be further complicated post-Scottish Independence vote in September 2014 (Chaney, 2011; Driver, 2011). The complexity of the above point with the changing nature of Parliamentary democracy in the United Kingdom, let alone abroad, has to be highlighted in continuing professional development for practitioners, because as I would argue citizenship teachers and lecturers need to know about it. As the DfE (2013b) Citizenship Programme of Study continues in Figure 7.1, pupils should also be taught:

- the different electoral systems used in and beyond the United Kingdom and action citizens can take in democratic and electoral processes to influence decisions locally, nationally and beyond;
- other systems and forms of government, both democratic and non-democratic, beyond the United Kingdom;
- local, regional and international governance and the United Kingdom's relations with the rest of Europe, the Commonwealth, the United Nations and the wider world;
- Human rights and international law;
- the legal system in the United Kingdom, different sources of law and how the law helps society deal with complex problems;
- diverse national, regional, religious and ethnic identities in the United Kingdom and the need for mutual respect and understanding;
- the different ways in which a citizen can contribute to the improvement of his or her community, to include the opportunity to participate actively in community volunteering, as well as other forms of responsible activity. (DfE, 2013b: 2–3)

Figure 7.1 Citizenship Programme of Study

The first two points in Figure 7.1 highlight the devolved political systems in the United Kingdom. International political systems remained undefined. The focus on Europe and the United Nations is globally focused as well as the point on human rights and international law (QCDA, 2009). Domestic law – which is highlighted in greater detail at Key Stage 3 (DfE, 2013c) is mentioned here. In relation to multiculturalism, we have diverse identities being recognized and the way in which citizens can contribute to community but it is based on 'responsible activity'. As raised earlier in the book, the term 'active responsibility', highlighted in previous education policy documents examined (DES, 1965; 1970), revolves around individual behaviour within the state and the citizenship curriculum is being taught yet again (QCDA, 2009) to deliver this objective.

The second document on Programmes of Study and Attainment Target Level Descriptors of Citizenship at Key Stage 4 (DfE, 2013c) also provides useful insights into what is meant by citizenship and how significantly it should be delivered that is taught in schools: 'Citizenship encourages [young people] . . . to take an interest in topical and controversial issues and to engage in discussion and debates. Pupils learn about their rights, responsibilities, duties and freedoms and about laws, justice and democracy' (DfE, 2013c: 9). The importance of citizenship issues relate to social justice, human rights, community cohesion and global interdependence but a key concept of citizenship relates only to justice (DfE, 2013c: 11) with the loss of the 'social'. As in Key Stage 3 (DfE, 2013b) the term justice has a more implied legal rather than social focus. Diversity is also one of the six key concepts of citizenship but is again vague in its definition, not encompassing a more specific social or cultural diversity explanation. 'The justice system' is also raised as a term in range and content which citizenship should include but 'social justice' is again not mentioned. The focus within citizenship range and content is more legal and economic rather than social and cultural. It is worth highlighting an explanatory note within the document on the economy in relation to citizenship: 'Students should consider the role of government in ensuring the business can flourish and citizens can prosper in a free and fair economy.' This comment then leads into a familiar education policy statement: 'The rights and responsibilities of consumers, employers and employees . . .' (DfE, 2013c: 13) are also highlighted. We have the familiar 'rights and responsibilities' of the individual, in this case being applied to economic measures. However, diversity is mentioned, as it was in the citizenship QCDA (2009) guidelines, but the tone of the following point is politically different than it was in 2009: Citizenship range and content should focus on:

> the origins and implications of diversity and the changing nature of society in the UK, including the perspectives and values that are shared or common, and the impact of migration and integration on identities, groups and communities. (DfE, 2013c: 13)

When analysing the above point, it is important to highlight 'the origins and implications' of diversity but the now non-statutory status of citizenship means that diversity teaching will depend on the individual school resources and whether there are teachers that can teach specific and general diversity studies and issues that concern the student body. 'Impact[s] of migration and integration . . .' are also significant because of the continuing changing nature of migration and consequent integrationist political reaction – see the section on the Merkel, Cameron and Clegg political speeches above – alongside the developing need to continually train professional practitioners to deliver contemporary and relevant curricula, in this case, to students within citizenship at Key Stage 4.

In Figure 7.2, curriculum opportunities for citizenship are highlighted in full and are done so when comparing and developing the information discussed at the end of Chapter 5 as well as the sections in Chapter 6 on the Diversity of Citizenship and the potential of citizenship education.

Citizenship – Curriculum Opportunities – the curriculum should provide opportunities for students to . . .

a. debate, in groups and whole-class discussions, topical and controversial issues, including those of concern to young people and their communities;

b. develop citizenship knowledge and understanding while using and applying citizenship skills;

c. work individually and in groups, taking on different roles and responsibilities;

d. participate in both school-based and community-based citizenship activities and reflect on their participation;

e. participate in different forms of individual and collective action, including decision-making and campaigning;

f. work with a range of community partners and organizations to address issues and problems in communities;

g. take into account legal, moral, economic, environmental, historical and social dimensions of different political problems and issues;

h. take into account a range of contexts, such as school, neighbourhood, local, regional, national, European, international and global, as relevant to different topics;

i. use and interpret different media and ICT both as sources of information and as a means of communicating ideas;

j. make links between citizenship and work in other subjects and areas of the curriculum. (DfE, 2013c: 14)

Figure 7.2 Citizenship – Curriculum Opportunities

I have argued (Race, 2011; 2012) that citizenship has the potential and possibility to provide a diverse, multicultural curriculum and Figure 7.2 does highlight the breath and range of the possibility. It would also be productive to develop the bullet points that were made on multicultural education practice at the end of Chapter 5 by examining the terminology used in Figure 7.2. Terms such as 'participate' can be added to the method bullet point in the list on multicultural education practice. 'Work with community partners' can be added to the Depth bullet point. 'The range of contexts' can be added to the reach point as well as the interpretations of media and Information and Communication Technology (ICT). As Stevenson (2014) suggests, the range of content needs to go beyond the domestic towards the international as ICT allows and should go beyond Key Stage 4. Figure 7.2 underlines the potential of citizenship curriculum and the possibilities of multicultural education practice in the bullet points which have been altered from those set out in Chapter 5 to highlight recent ideas and thinking:

- Method – how practice allows students to talk, think, reflect and participate within the classroom and wider communities;
- Depth – practice needs to avoid the tokenistic. Stereotyping needs to be avoided at all costs. Working in the classroom and within communities can increase understandings of the social and cultural, as well as the economic and legal;
- Reach – practice needs to be international rather than nation. A range of global contexts needs to be analysed and examined with interpretations of media through ICT, as well as a more multicultural and intersectional focus on events.

Reflective Exercise

- How can a citizenship Programme of Study evolve?
- What citizenship curriculum opportunities in terms of delivery and content should students in schools be given?

Summary

It would perhaps seem naïve and unrealistic to state that multicultural citizenship is possible when this chapter has acknowledged a shift from multicultural to integrationist citizenship. Despite what multiculturalism offers and what Kymlicka argues in relation to multicultural citizenship that is a focus and distinction between national minorities and ethnic differences, what is as significant in the context of this chapter, is how great a degree state intervention has increased within citizenship education policy in England. Acknowledging how difficult it actually is for the state to shape or influence a complex subject like cultural diversity within citizenship, the next stage of understanding is how the state through policy-making then influences the response of individuals and groups. Moreover, with Parekh (2008) and Banks (2014) underlining the continued need for multicultural education, we witness Merkel and Cameron calling for more integrationist policies. Joppke (2012) highlights the important debate between civic integration and European citizenship, a political debate, seemingly shifting back towards a more national, integrationist focus after the May 2014 European Elections.

This also highlights a conceptual movement from multicultural to integrationist citizenship. Despite Merkel and Clegg recognizing multiculturalism and cultural diversity, all three speeches in this chapter highlight more integrationist political thinking. Latour (2012) highlights the disagreements between Clegg and Cameron but Coalition education policy in England is geared more towards integrationist policy (Race, 2012; 2014). Whether an idea like the 'good citizen' (Merry, 2013) is possible is debatable because one way of promoting this is through a citizenship education curriculum. When reflecting on the three practical bullet points in the previous section of method, reach and depth, how can this shape current professional practice? This could theoretically be more multiculturally focused than integrationist but this is dependent on the politics of the government in power.

Within an English context, OFSTED (2013) provides an account of how citizenship between 2009–2012 is being consolidated within English Schools. Within primary schools, OFSTED (ibid.) show citizenship is 'thriving', but in the few weaker primary schools visited by the Inspectorate, 'poor curriculum planning means there were gaps in pupils' knowledge and understanding'. In secondary schools in England, citizenship education was 'stronger' than previous evidence collected by OFSTED in 2010 (ibid.). Provision in the weaker secondary schools was characterized by insufficient teaching time, teachers' lack of subject expertise and a lack of systems that could identify and address important weaknesses (OFSTED, 2013: 4; Race, 2014). This concurs with empirical evidence collected in this book and evidence from the literature with the need for continuing professional development not only in citizenship but other subjects within the national curriculum (CfBT / British Council, 2014). Moreover, the other key findings from the first edition of this book also still hold that is the conceptual requirement to increase our understandings of integration, highlighted in this chapter by the movement from multicultural to integrationist citizenship with the demand for more diversity training to understand changing cultural diversity which ties in with continuing professional development. The new finding which we need to take forward is the need to reflect on curriculum content and curriculum delivery in all subjects for example how education subjects like citizenship and MFL are politically created, shaped by changing politics and politically evolve over time. Figures 7.1. and 7.2. highlight how the citizenship curriculum has changed from a statutory curriculum that was more culturally diverse (QCDA, 2009) – see the previous chapter – to a curriculum with less opportunities to examine cultural diversity (DfE, 2013b; 2013c) at Key Stages 3 and 4 which is now simply more integrationist than multicultural. That process occurred with a change of government in England in 2010. However, despite this change in education policy, the need to continue to advocate multicultural education practice in not only citizenship and MFL but in all subjects and within all age ranges, remains the key finding and idea of this book.

Useful websites

Department for Education (DfE)
    www.education.gov.uk/
Office for Standards in Education (OFSTED)
    www.ofsted.gov.uk/
Office of Qualifications and Examinations Regulation (OfQual)
    http://ofqual.gov.uk/

Bibliography

Adam-Moodley, K. (1986) 'The Politics of Education in Three Multicultural Societies: Germany, South Africa and Canada', in Samuda, R. J. and Kong, S. L. (eds) *Multicultural Education. Programmes and Methods*, Toronto: Toronto University Press, 1–14.

Albrecht, F. (2007) 'Islamic Religious Education in Western Europe: Models of Integration and the German Approach', *Journal of Muslim Minority Affairs*, 27, 2, 215–39.

Aldrich, R. (1982) *An Introduction to the History of Education*, London: Hodder and Stoughton.

Aldrich, R. (ed.) (2002) *A Century of Education*, London: RoutledgeFalmer.

Alred, G., Byram, M. and Fleming, M. (2006) *Education for Intercultural Citizenship. Concepts and Comparisons*, Clevedon: Multilingual Matters.

Annette, J. (2005) 'Faith Schools and Communities: Communitarianism, Social Capital and Citizenship', in Gardner, R., Cairns, J. and Lawton, D. (eds) *Faith Schools. Consensus or Conflict?* Abingdon: RoutledgeFalmer, 191–201.

Anthias, F. (2012) 'Intersectional What? Social Divisions, Intersectionality and Levels of Analysis', *Ethnicities*, 13, 1, 3–19.

Anthias, F. and Yuval-Davies, N. (1993) *Racialised Boundaries: Race, Nation, Gender, Colour and Class and the Anti-Racist Struggle*, London: Routledge.

Arber, R. (2008) *Race, Ethnicity and Education in Globalised Times*, New York: Springer.

Archer, L. and Francis, B. (2007) *Understanding Minority Ethnic Achievement. Race, Gender, Class and 'Success'*, London: Routledge.

Armstrong, C. (2006) *Rethinking Equality: The Challenge of Equal Citizenship*, Manchester: Manchester University Press.

Aughey, A. (2007) *The Politics of Englishness*, Manchester: Manchester University Press.

Baber, H. E. (2008) *The Multicultural Mystique. The Liberal Case against Diversity*, New York: Prometheus Books.

Back, L. (2005) '"Home from Home": Youth, Belonging and Place', in Alexander, C. and Knowles, C. (eds) *Making Race Matter. Bodies, Spaces & Identity*, Houndsmills: Palgrave Macmillan, 19–41.

Baker, D. P. and LeTendre, G. K. (2005) *National Differences, Global Similarities. World Culture and the Future of Schooling*, Stanford: Stanford University Press.

Ball, S. J. (2003) *Class Struggles and the Education Market. The Middle Classes and Social Advantage*, London: RoutledgeFalmer.

Ball, S. J. (2007) *Education PLC. Understanding Private Sector Participation in Public Sector Education*, London: Routledge.

Ball, S. J. (2008) *The Education Debate*, Bristol: Policy Press.

Ball, S. J. (2nd ed.) (2013) *The Education Debate*, Bristol: Policy Press.

Banks, C. A. M. (2005) *Improving Multicultural Education. Lessons from the Intergroup Education Movement*, New York: Teachers College Press.

Banks, C. A. M. and Esposito, J. (2009) 'Cultural Capital', in Provenzo, E. F. (ed.) *Encyclopedia of the Social and Cultural Foundations of Education, Volume 1,* Sage: Thousand Oaks, 2009.

Banks, J. A. (1986) 'Multicultural Education and Its Critics: Britain and the United States', in Modgil, S., Verma, G. K., Mallick, K. and Modgil, C. (eds) *Multicultural Education. The Interminable Debate,* Lewes: Falmer Press, 221–32.

Banks, J. A. (1992) 'Multicultural Education: Approaches, Developments and Dimensions', in Lynch, J., Modgil, C. and Modgil, S. (eds) *Cultural Diversity and The Schools. Volume 1. Education for Cultural Diversity Convergence and Divergence,* London: Falmer Press, 83–94.

Banks, J. A. (1993) 'Education and Cultural Diversity in the United States', in Fyfe, A. and Figueroa, P. (eds) *Education for Cultural Diversity. The Challenge for a New Era,* London: Routledge, 49–68.

Banks, J. A. (4th ed.) (2001) *Cultural Diversity and Education. Foundations, Curriculum, and Teaching,* Boston: Allyn and Bacon.

Banks, J. A. (ed.) (2004) *Diversity and Citizenship Education,* San Francisco: Jossey-Bass.

Banks, J. A. (2005) 'The Social Construction of Difference and the Quest for Educational Equality', in Leonardo, Z. (ed.) *Critical Pedagogy and Race,* Oxford: Blackwell, 93–110.

Banks, J. A. (2nd ed.) (2007) *Educating Citizens in a Multicultural Society,* New York: Teachers College Press.

Banks, J. A. (ed.) (2009) *The Routledge International Companion to Multicultural Education,* Abingdon: Routledge.

Banks, J. A. (5th ed.) (2014) *An Introduction of Multicultural Education,* Boston: Pearson Education.

Banks, J. A. and Banks, C. A. M. (eds) (6th ed.) (2007) *Multicultural Education: Issues and Perspectives,* New Jersey: Wiley.

Baumann, G. (1996) *Contesting Culture. Discourses of Identity in Multi-ethnic London,* Cambridge: Cambridge University Press.

Beck, U. (2009) *World at Risk,* Cambridge: Polity Press.

Ben-Porath, S. R. (2006) *Citizenship Under Fire. Democratic Education in Times of Conflict,* Princeton: Princeton University Press.

Best, R. (ed.) (2000) *Education for Spiritual, Moral, Social and Cultural Development,* London: Continuum.

Best, R., Lang, P., Lodge, C. and Watkins, C. (eds) (1995) *Pastoral Care and Personal-Social Education. Entitlement and Provision,* London: Continuum.

Bhattacharya, N. (2009) 'Teaching History in Schools: The Politics of Textbooks in India', *History Workshop Journal,* 67, 1, 99–110.

Bhavnani, R., Mirza, H. S. and Meetoon, V. (2005) *Tackling the Roots of Racism. Lessons for Success,* Bristol: Policy Press.

Bhopal, K. and Preston, J. (eds) (2012) *Intersectionality and 'Race' in Education,* London: Routledge.

Biles, J., Burstein, M. and Frideres, J. (eds) (2008) *Immigration and Integration in Canada,* Montreal: McGill-Queen's University Press.

Blair, M. (2008) '"Whiteness" as Institutionalized Racism as Conspiracy: Understanding the Paradigm', *Educational Review,* 60, 3, 249–51.

Bleich, E. (2009) 'Muslims and the State in the Post 9/11 Era: Introduction', *Journal of Ethnic and Migration Studies,* 35, 3, 353–60.

Bloom, A. (2008) 'Teaching Diversity Is the Way to Prevent Terrorism, Says Lecturer', *Times Educational Supplement*, 4th April, Article accessible from, www.tes.co.uk/article.aspx?storycode=2602484, last accessed 19th August 2009.

Blunkett, D. (1995) *On a Clear Day: An Autobiography*, London: Michael O'Mara Books.

Bolton, G. (3rd ed.) (2010) *Reflective Practice. Writing & Professional Development*, London: Sage.

Bourdieu, P. (2004) *Science of Science and Reflexivity*, Cambridge: Polity Press.

Bourdieu, P. (2005) *The Social Structures of the Economy*, Cambridge: Polity Press.

Bourdieu, P. (2010) *Distinction: A Social Critique of the Judgement of Taste*, London: Routledge.

Bourdieu, P. and Passeron, J.-C. (2nd ed.) (1990) *Reproduction in Education, Society and Culture*, London: Sage.

Bowen, J. R. (2007) *Why the French Don't Like Headscarves. Islam, the State, and Public Space*, Princeton: Princeton University Press.

Brah, A. (1992) 'Difference, Diversity and Differentiation', in Donald, J. and Rattansi, A. (eds) *'Race', Culture and Difference*, Milton Keynes: Sage in association with Open University Press, 126, 148.

British Broadcasting Company (BBC) (2010) 'Merkel Says German Multicultural Society Has Failed', http://www.bbc.co.uk/news/world-europe-11559451, last accessed 14th March 2014.

Brooks, D. (2003) *Steve and Me. My Friendship with Stephen Lawrence and the Search for Justice*, London: Abacus.

Bryson, B. (2005) *Making Multiculturalism. Boundaries and Meaning in U.S. English Departments*, Stanford: Stanford University Press.

Burton, D. and Bartlett, S. (2005) *Practitioner Research for Teachers*, London: Paul Chapman.

Callan, E. (2007) *Creating Citizens. Political Education and Liberal Democracy*, Oxford: Clarendon Press.

Cameron, D. (2011) PM Speech at Munich Security Conference – 5th February 2011 https://www.gov.uk/government/speeches/pms-speech-at-munich-security-conference, last acceessed 14th March 2014.

Canadian Department of the Secretary of State (CDSoS) (1987) *Multiculturalism: Being Canadian*, Ottawa: Supply and Services, Canada.

Canadian Ministry of State for Multiculturalism and Citizenship (CMoSMC) (1991) *Multiculturalism: What Is It Really About?* Ottawa: Supply and Services, Canada.

Cantle, T. (2008) *Community Cohesion. A New Framework for Race and Diversity*, Houndsmills: Palgrave Macmillan.

Castelli, M. and Trevathan, A. (2006) 'The English Public Space: Developing Spirituality in English Muslim schools', in Johnson, H. (ed.) *Reflecting on Faith Schools*, Abingdon: Routledge, 9–18.

Centre for British Teachers (CfBT) / British Council (2014) *Language Trends 2013 /14. The State of Language Learning in Primary and Secondary Schools in England*, http://www.britishcouncil.org/sites/britishcouncil.uk2/files/language-trends-survey-2014.pdf, last accessed 10th April 2014.

Chaney, P. (2011) 'Education, Equality and Human Rights: Exploring the Impact of Devolution in the UK', *Critical Social Policy*, 31, 3, 431–53.

Citizenship and Immigration Canada (CIC) (2009) 'What is Multiculturalism?' www.cic.gc.ca/multi/multi-eng.asp, last accessed 24th August 2009.

Clegg, N. (2011) 'An Open, Confident Society: The application of Muscular Liberalism in a Multicultural Society – 3rd March 2011 – https://www.gov.uk/government/speeches/deputy-prime-ministers-speech-on-the-open-confident-society, last accessed 14th March 2014.

Coelho, E. (1998) *Teaching and Learning in Multicultural Schools. An Integrated Approach*, Clevedon: Multilingual Matters.

Cohen, L. and Manion, L. (1983) *Multicultural Classrooms*, London: Croon Helm.

Collinson, V., Kozina, E., Yu-Hao, K. L., Matherson, I., Newcombe, L. and Zogla, I. (2009) 'Professional Development for Teachers: A World of Change', *European Journal of Teacher Education*, 32, 1, 3–19.

Commission on Integration and Cohesion (CIC) (2007) *Our Shared Vision*, Wetherby, Crown Copyright, Full text available, at, http://collections.europarchive.org/tna/20080726153624/http://www.integrationandcohesion.org.uk/~/media/assets/www.integrationandcohesion.org.uk/ our_shared_future%20pdf.ashx, last accessed 15th August 2009.

Connolly, P. (1998) *Racism, Gender Identities and Young Children. Social Relations in a Multi-Ethnic, Inner-City Primary School*, London: Routledge.

Cornbleth, C. (2008) *Diversity and the New Teacher: Learning from Experience in Urban Schools*, New York: Teachers College Press.

Corson, D. (1998) *Changing Education for Diversity*, Buckingham: Open University Press.

Cremin, H. and Warwick, P. (2008) 'Multiculturalism is Dead: Long Live Community Cohesion? A Case Study of an Educational Methodology to Empower Young People as Global Citizens', *Research in Comparative and International Education*, 3, 1, 36–49.

Crick, B. (1990) *Political Thoughts and Polemics*, Edinburgh: Edinburgh University Press.

Crick, B. (2008) 'Citizenship, Diversity and National Identity', *London Review of Education*, 6, 1, 31–37.

Crowder, G. (2013) *Theories of Multiculturalism. An Introduction*, Cambridge:, Polity Press.

Davies, G. (1986) 'Strategies for Change', in Arora, R. and Duncan, C. (eds) *Multicultural Education. Towards Good Practice*, London: Routledge & Kegan Paul, 9–24.

Day, R. J. F. (2002) *Multiculturalism and the History of Canadian Diversity*, Toronto: University of Toronto Press.

Dei, G. J. S. (2005) 'Critical Issues in Anti-Racist Methodologies', in Dei, G. J. S. and Johal, G. S. (eds) *Critical Issues in Anti-Racist Methodologies*, New York: Peter Lang, 1–28.

Delgardo, R. and Stefanic, J. (2001) *Critical Race Theory: An Introduction*, New York: New York University Press.

Dent, H. C. (9th ed.) (1962) *The Education Act 1944*, London: University of London Press.

Department for Children, Schools and Families (DCSF) (2007) 'Faith in the System: The Role of Schools with a Religious Character in English Education and Society', full text available at, http://publications. dcsf.gov.uk/eOrderingDownload/FaithInTheSystem.pdf, last accessed 19th August 2009.

Department for Education (DfE) (2011) Education Act 2011 http://www.legislation.gov.uk/ukpga/2011/21/contents/enacted, last accessed 10th April 2014.

DfE (2013a) The Equality Act 2010. Departmental Advice for School Leaders, School Staff and Governing Bodies in Maintained Schools and Academies, February 2013, https://www.gov.uk/

government/uploads/system/uploads/attachment_data/file/269341/Equality_Act_2010_-_advice.pdf, last accessed 10th April 2014.

DfE (2013b) Citizenship Programmes of Study: Key Stages 3 and 4. National Curriculum in England, https://www.gov.uk/government/uploads/system/uploads/attachment_data/file/239060/SECONDARY_national_curriculum_-_Citizenship.pdf, last accessed 11th April 2014.

DfE (2013c) Citizenship – Schools – Key Stage 3 and 4, https://www.gov.uk/government/uploads/system/uploads/attachment_data/file/239060/SECONDARY_national_curriculum_-_Citizenship.pdf, last accessed 11th April 2014.

Department for Education and Employment (DfEE) (2001) *Schools – Building on Success*, London: DfEE.

Department for Education and Skills (DfES (2002) *Schools Achieving Success,* Annesley, DfES. Full text available at, www.archive.official-documents.co.uk/document/cm52/5230/5230.pdf, last accessed 19th August 2009.

Department of Education and Science (DES) (1967) *Report of the Central Advisory Council for Education, Children and Their Primary* Schools (the Plowden Report). Full text available from the Education in England website at, www.dg.dial.pipex.com/documents/plowden.shtml, last accessed 10th July 2009.

DES (1971) 'The Education of Immigrants', London: HMSO. DES (1977) 'Education in Schools', London: HMSO.

DES (1981) 'West Indian Children in Our Schools' (The Rampton Report), London: HMSO.

DES (1985) 'Education for All' (The Swann Report), London: HMSO.

DES (1988) 'Education Reform Act' Chapter 40, Full text available at, www.opsi.gov.uk/acts/acts1988/ukpga_19880040_en_1, last accessed 26th August 2009.

DfES (2004) *Every Child Matters: Change for Children in Schools*, London: DfES.

DfES (2006) *The Education and Inspections Act*, Chapter 40, London, HMSO, Full text available at, www.opsi.gov.uk/acts/acts2006/pdf/ukpga_20060040_en.pdf, last accessed 17th August 2009.

DfES (2007) *Diversity and Citizenship Curriculum Review*, London, DfES. Full text available at, http://publications.teachernet.gov.uk/eOrderingDownload/DfES_Diversity_&_Citizenship.pdf, last accessed 15th August 2009.

Dhingra, P. (2007) *Managing Multicultural Lives. Asian-American Professionals and the Challenge of Multiple Identities*, Stanford: Stanford University Press.

Dlamini, S. N. and Matinovic, D. (2007) 'In Pursuit of Being Canadian: Examining the Challenges of Culturally Relevant Education in Teacher Education Programs', *Race, Ethnicity and Education*, 10, 2, 155–75.

Driver, S. (2011) *Understanding British Party Politics*, Cambridge: Polity Press.

Du Gay, P. (2007) *Organizing Identity,* London: Sage.

Eade, J., Barrett, M., Flood, C. and Race, R. (eds) (2008) *Advancing Multiculturalism, Post 7/7*, Newcastle-Upon-Tyne: Cambridge Scholars Publishing.

Elliot, A. and du Gay, P. (2009) *Identity in Question*, London: Sage.

Equality Act (2010) Chapter 15. (2010) Available at: http://www.legislation.gov.uk/ukpga/2010/15/contents, last accessed 10th April 2014.

Fairclough, A. (2007) *A Class of Their Own. Black Teachers in the Segregated South*, Harvard: Harvard University Press.

Figueroa, P. (1991) *Education and the Social Construction of 'Race'*, New York: Routledge.

Finney, N. and Simpson, L. (2009) *'Sleepwalking to Segregation?' Challenging Myths about Race and Migration*, Bristol: Policy Press.

Flint, J. (2007) 'Faith Schools, Multiculturalism and Community Cohesion: Muslim and Roman Catholic State Schools in England and Scotland', *Policy and Politics*, 35, 2, 251–68.

Fook, J. and Gardner, F. (2007) *Practising Critical Reflection. A Resource Handbook*, Maidenhead: McGraw-Hill Education.

Forrester, D. and Harwin, J. (2008) 'Parental Substance Misuse and Child Welfare: Outcomes for Children Two Years After Referral', *British Journal of Social Work*, 38, 8, 1518–35.

Fyfe, A. (1993) 'Multicultural or Anti-Racist Education: The Irrelevant Debate', in Fyfe, A. and Figueroa, P. (eds) *Education for Cultural Diversity. The Challenge for a New Era*, London: Routledge, 37–48.

Gallagher, T. (2004) *Education in Divided Societies*, Houndsmills: Palgrave Macmillan.

Galton, M. and MacBeath, J. (2008) *Teachers Under Pressure*, London: National Union of Teachers and Sage.

Gardner, R. (2005) 'Faith Schools Now: An Overview', in Gardner, R., Cairns, J. and Lawton, D. (eds) *Faith Schools. Consensus or Conflict?* Abingdon: RoutledgeFalmer, 7–13.

Gause, C. P. (2008) *Integration Matters. Navigating Identity, Culture, and Resistance*, New York: Peter Lang.

Gay, G. (2nd ed.) (2010) *Culturally Responsive Teaching. Theory, Research, and Practice*, New York: Teachers College Press.

Geddes, A. (2nd ed.) (2008) *Immigration and European Integration. Beyond Fortress Europe*, Manchester: Manchester University Press.

Gereluk, D. (2006) *Education and Community*, London: Continuum.

Gereluk, D. (2008) *Symbolic Clothing in Schools. What Should be Worn and Why*, London: Continuum.

Gereluk, D. and Race, R. (2007) 'Multicultural Tensions in England, France and Canada: Contrasting Approaches and Consequences', *International Studies in Sociology of Education*, 17, 1 & 2, 113–29.

Gergen, K. J. and Gergen, M. M. (2009) 'Social Constructionism', in Given, L. M. (ed.) *The Sage Encyclopedia of Qualitative Research Methods*, Thousand Oaks: Sage, 816–20.

Gewirtz, S. (2006) 'Towards a Contextualized Analysis of Social Justice in Education', in Sardoc, M. (ed.) *Citizenship, Inclusion and Democracy. A Symposium on Iris Marion Young*, Oxford: Blackwell, 67–80.

Giddens, A. (1998) *The Third Way. The Renewal of Social Democracy*, Cambridge: Polity Press.

Giddens, A. (2007) *Over to You, Mr. Brown*, Cambridge: Polity Press.

Gill, D., Mayor, B. and Blair, M. (eds) (1992) *Racism and Education. Structures and Strategies*, Milton Keynes: Sage in association with Open University Press.

Gillborn, D. (1990) *Race, Ethnicity and Education: Teaching and Learning in Multi-ethnic Schools*, London: Routledge.

Gillborn, D. (1995) *Racism and Antiracism in Schools. Theory, Policy, Practice*, Buckingham: Open University Press.

Gillborn, D. (2001) 'Racism, Policy and the (Mis)education of Black Children', in Majors, R. (ed.) *Educating Our Black Children. New Directions and Radical Approaches*, London: Routledge, 13–27.

Gillborn, D. (2005) 'Anti-racism: From Policy to Praxis', in Leonardo, Z. (ed.) *Critical Pedagogy and Race*, Oxford: Blackwell, 111–26.

Gillborn, D. (2008a) *Racism and Education. Coincidence or Conspiracy?* London: Routledge.

Gillborn, D. (2008b) 'Tony Blair and the Politics of Race in Education: Whiteness, *Doublethink* and New Labour', *Oxford Review of Education*, 34, 6, 713–25.

Gilroy, P. (1992) *There Ain't No Black in the Union Jack*, London: Routledge.

Gilroy, P. (2006) 'Multiculturalism and Post-colonial Theory', in Dryzek, J. S., Hong, B. and Phillips, A. (eds) *The Oxford Handbook of Political Theory*, Oxford: Oxford University Press, 656–76.

Goldstein, H. (2008) 'Evidence and Education Policy – Some Reflections and Allegations', *Cambridge Journal of Education*, 38, 3, 393–400.

Gomberg, P. (2007) *How to Make Opportunity Equal. Race and Contributive Justice*, Oxford: Blackwell.

Goodhart, D. (2006) 'National Anxieties', *Prospect*, Number 123, For full text see, www.prospectmaga-zine.co.uk/2006/06/nationalanxieties/, last accessed 27th August 2009.

Gordon, P. and Lawton, D. (2003) *Dictionary of British Education*, London: Woburn Press.

Grace, G. (2003) 'Educational Studies and Faith-Based Schooling: Moving from Prejudice to Evidence-based Argument', *British Journal of Educational Studies*, 51, 2, 149–67.

Grant, C. A. (1999) 'Personal and Intellectual Motivation for Working from the Margin', in Grant, C. A. (ed.) *Multicultural Research. A Reflective Engagement with Race, Gender and Sexual Orientation*, London: Falmer Press, 157–67.

Grant, C. A. (2006) 'Multiculturalism, Race and the Public Interest: Hanging on to Great–Great Granddaddy's Legacy', in Ladson-Billings, G. and Tate, W. F. (eds) *Education Research in the Public Interest*, New York: Teachers College Press, 158–72.

Green, A. (1991) *Education and State Formation. The Rise of Education Systems in England, France and the USA*, Basingstoke: Palgrave Macmillan, 130–70.

Griffin, R. (2006) 'Introduction and Overview', in Griffin, R. (ed.) *Education in the Muslim World: Different Perspectives*, Oxford: Symposium Books, 9–24.

Griffiths, M. (2003) *Action for Social Justice in Education*, Maidenhead: Open University Press.

Grosvenor, I. (1997) *Assimilating Identities. Racism and Educational Policy in Post 1945 Britain*, London: Lawrence & Wishart.

Guibernau, M. (2007) *The Identity of Nations*, Cambridge: Polity Press.

Gundara, J. (1986) 'Education for a Multicultural Society', in Gundara, J., Jones, C. and Kimberley, K. (eds) *Racism, Diversity and Education*, London: Hodder and Stoughton, 4–27.

Gundara, J. (2000) *Interculturalism Education and Inclusion*, London: Paul Chapman Publishing.

Gutierrez, K. D. and Rogaff, B. (2009) 'Cultural Ways of Learning', in Daniels, H., Lauder, H. and Porter, J. with Sarah Hartshorn (eds) *Knowledge, Values and Educational Policy: A Critical Perspective*, London: Routledge, 114–25.

Halsey, A. H. (1978) *Change in British Society. Based on the Reith Lectures*, Oxford: Oxford University Press.

Halstead, M. J. (2007) 'Islamic Values: A Distinctive Framework for Moral Education?', *Journal of Moral Education*, 36, 3, 283–96.

Hantrais, L. (2009) *International Comparative Research: Theory, Methods and Practice*, Houndsmills: Palgrave Macmillan.

Harrison, J. (2008) 'Professional Development and the Reflective Practitioner', in Dymoke, S. and Harrison, J. (eds) *Reflective Teaching & Learning*, London: Sage, 7–44.

Harty, S. and Murphy, M. (2005) *In Defence of Multicultural Citizenship*, Cardiff: University of Wales Press.

Heater, D. (2001) 'The History of Citizenship Education in England', *The Curriculum Journal*, 12, 1, 103–23.

Held, D. and McGrew, A. (eds) (2007) *Globalization Theory. Approaches and Controversies*, Cambridge: Polity Press.

Hewitt, R. (2005) *White Blacklash and the Politics of Multiculturalism*, Cambridge: Cambridge University Press.

Hicks, G. (2007) *One Unknown*, London: Pan Macmillan.

Home Office (1999) Recommendations from the Stephen Lawrence Inquiry, www.archive.official-documents.co.uk/document/cm42/4262/sli-47.htm, last accessed 2nd September 2010.

Home Office (2001) *Community Cohesion: A Report of the Independent Review Team* (The Cantle Report), London: HMSO.

Home Office (2003) *Every Child Matters*, London: HMSO.

Honeyford, R. (1988) *Integration or Disintegration?* London: Claridge Press.

House of Commons (HoC) (2007) *The Governance of Britain*, CM7170, London, HMSO, Full text available at, www.official-documents.gov.uk/document/cm71/7170/7170.pdf, last accessed 15th August 2009.

Howard, T. C. (2010) *Why Race and Culture Matter in Schools. Closing the Achievement Gap in America's Classrooms*, New York: Teachers College Press.

Huat, C. M. and Kerry, T. (2008) *International Perspectives on Education*, London: Continuum.

Ibanez-Martin, J. A. (1996) 'Multiculturalism, Identity and Unity', in Amilburu, M. G. (ed.) *Education, The State and The Multicultural Challenge*, Eunsa: Pamplona, 89–100.

Jackson, R. (2001) 'Editorial', *British Journal of Religious Education*, 24, 1, 2–7.

Jackson, R. (2004) *Rethinking Religious Education and Plurality. Issues in Diversity and Pedagogy*, London: RoutledgeFalmer.

Jackson, R. (2006) 'Intercultural Education and Religious Education: A Changing Relationship' in Bates, D., Durka, G. and Schweitzer, F. (eds) *Education, Religion and Society. Essays in Honour of John M. Hull*, London: Routledge, 49–61.

Jenkins, R. (1997) *Rethinking Ethnicity. Arguments and Explorations*, London: Sage.

John, G. (2005) 'Parental and Community Involvement in Education: Time to Get the Balance Right', in Richardson, B. (ed.) *Tell It Like It Is: How Our Schools Fail Black Children*, Stoke-on-Trent: Trentham Books, 97–107.

Johnson, G. F. and Enomoto, R. (eds) (2007) *Race, Racialization, and Antiracism in Canada and Beyond*, Toronto: University of Toronto Press.

Joppke, C. (2010) *Citizenship and Immigration*, Cambridge: Polity Press.

Joppke, C. (2012) *The Role of the State in Cultural Integration: Trends, Challenges, and Ways Ahead*, http://www.migrationpolicy.org/research/TCM-state-role-in-cultural-integration, last accessed 30th April 2014.

Judge, H. (2002) *Faith-based Schools and the State. Catholics in America, France and England*, Oxford: Symposium Books.

Keating, A. (2009) 'Educating Europe's Citizens: Moving from National to Post-national Models of Educating for European Citizenship', *Citizenship Studies*, 13, 2, 135–51.

Keating, A. and Benton, T. (2013) 'Creating Cohesive Citizens in England? Exploring the Role of Diversity. Deprivation and Democratic Climate at School', *Education, Citizenship and Social Justice*, 8, 2, 165–84.

Khuram, K. (2007) 'An Islamic Consideration of Western Moral Education: An Exploration of the Individual', *Journal of Moral Education*, 36, 3, 297–308.

Kincheloe, J. L. and Steinberg, S. R. (1997) *Changing Multiculturalism*, Maidenhead: Open University Press.

Kymlicka, W. (1995) *Multicultural Citizenship. A Liberal Theory of Minority Rights*, Oxford: Clarendon Press.

Kymlicka, W. (2007) *Multicultural Odysseys. Navigating the New International Politics of Diversity*, Oxford: Oxford University Press.

Kymlicka, W. (2012) *Multiculturalism: Success, Failure, and the Future*, http://www.migrationpolicy. org/research/TCM-multiculturalism-success-failure, last accessed 30th April 2014.

Ladson-Billings, G. (1992) 'Culturally Relevant Teaching: The Key to Making Multicultural Education Work', in Grant, C. A. (ed.) *Research and Multicultural Education: From the Margins to the Mainstream*, London: Falmer Press, 106–21.

Ladson-Billings, G. (2004) 'Just What is Critical Race Theory and What's It Doing in a *Nice* Field Like Education?', in Ladson-Billings, G. and Gillborn, D. (eds) *The RoutledgeFalmer Reader in Multicultural Education*, London: RoutledgeFalmer, 49–68.

Lanz, S. (2010) 'The German Sonderweg: Multiculturalism as 'Racism with a Distance', in Silj, A. (ed.) *European Multiculturalism Revisited*, London: Zed Books, 105–46.

Latour, V. (2012) 'Muscular Liberalism': Surviving Multiculturalism? A Historical and Political Contextualisation of David Cameron's Munich Speech', *Open Edition*, Volume 12, http://osb.revues. org/1355, last accessed 14th March 2012.

Lauder, H., Brown, P., Dillabough, J.-A. and Halsey, A. H. (2006) *Education, Globalization and Social Change*, Oxford: Oxford University Press.

Lea, V. and Sims, E. J. (2008) 'Afterword – Educulturalism in the Service of Social Justice Activism', in Lea, V. and Sims, E. J. (eds) *Undoing Whiteness in the Classroom. Critical Educational Teaching Approaches for Social Justice Activism*, New York: Peter Lang, 255–72.

Leach, P. (2009) *Child Care Today. What We Know and What We Need to Know*, Cambridge: Polity Press.

Lechner, F. J. (2009) *Globalization: The Making of World Society*, Oxford: Wiley-Blackwell.

Levine-Rasky, C. and Ringrose, J. (2009) 'Theorizing Psychosocial Processes in Canadian, Middle-class, Jewish Mothers' School Choice', *Journal of Education Policy*, 24, 3, 255–69.

Levy, J. T. (2000) *The Multiculturalism of Fear*, Oxford: Oxford University Press.

Lieberman, A. and Miller, L. (2008) 'Reflecting on the Themes of Context, Commitment, Capacity, Context, and Challenge', in Lieberman, A. and Miller, L. (eds) *Teachers in Professional Communities. Improving Teaching and Learning*, New York: Teachers College Press, 97–106.

Lister, M. and Pia, E. (2008) *Citizenship in Contemporary Europe*, Edinburgh: Edinburgh University Press.

Livingstone, S. (2009) *Children and the Internet*, Cambridge: Polity Press.

Lott, B. (2010) *Multiculturalism and Diversity. A Social Psychological Perspective*. Oxford: Wiley- Blackwell.

Lynch, J. (1989) 'International Interdependence: Swann's Contribution', in Verma, G. K. (ed.) *Education for All, A Landmark in Pluralism*, Lewes: Falmer Press, 118–31.

Lyon, D. (2009) *Identifying Citizens. ID Cards as Surveillance*, Cambridge: Polity Press.

Mac an Ghaill, M. (1988) *Young, Gifted and Black*, Milton Keynes: Open University Press.

Macdonald, I., Bhavnani, R., Khan, L. and John, G. (1989) *Murder in the Playground. The Report of the Macdonald Inquiry into Racism and Racial Violence in Manchester Schools*, London: Longsight Press.

Macintyre, S. and Simpson, N. (2009) 'Consensus and Division in Australian Citizenship Education', *Citizenship Studies*, 13, 2, 121–34.

MacPherson, W. (1999) 'The Stephen Lawrence Inquiry', CM 4246-I, London: The Stationery Office, available at, www.archive.offical-documents.co.uk/document/cm42/42624262.htm, last accessed 3rd July 2009.

Mahamdallie, H. (ed.) (2011) *Defending Multiculturalism: A Guide for the Movement*, London: Bookmarks Publications.

Martinez-Torteya, C., Bogat, A., von Eye, A. and Levendosky, A. A. (2009) 'Resilience Among Children Exposed to Domestic Violence: The Role of Risk and Protective Factors', *Child Development*, 80, 2, 562–77.

Mason, D. (1995) *Race & Ethnicity in Modern Britain*, Oxford: Oxford University Press.

Mason, D. (2003) 'Introduction', in Mason, D. (ed.) *Explaining Ethnic Differences. Changing Patterns of Disadvantage in Britain*, Bristol: Policy Press, 1–8.

Masselos, J. (2009) 'Raj Rhapsodies, Tourism, Heritage and the Seduction of History', *Cultural and Social History*, 6, 2, 246–47.

Massey, D. and Fischer, M. (2006) 'The Effect of Childhood Segregation on Minority Academic Performance at Selective Colleges', *Ethnic and Racial Studies*, 29, 1, 1–26.

May, S. (1998) 'Critical Multiculturalism and Cultural Difference: Avoiding Essentialism', in May, S. (ed.) *Critical Multiculturalism. Rethinking Multicultural and Antiracist Education*, London: Falmer Press, 11–41.

McCulloch, G. (2008) 'Meritocracy', in McCulloch, G. and Crook, D. (eds) *The Routledge International Encyclopedia of Education*, London: Routledge, 382–83.

McKinney, S. (2004) 'Jewish Education and Formation in Glasgow: A Case Study', *Journal of Beliefs and Values*, 25, 1, 31–41.

McKinney, S. (2008) 'Mapping the Debate on Faith Schooling in England', in Mckinney, S. (ed.) *Faith Schools in the Twenty-First Century*, Edinburgh: Dunedin Academic Press, 1–14.

McLaughlin, T. H. (2000) 'Citizenship Education in England: The Crick Report and Beyond', *Journal of Philosophy of Education*, 34, 4, 541–70.

Meier, D. (2002) *The Power of Their Ideas. Lessons for America from a Small School in Harlem*, Boston: Beacon Press.

Merry, M. S. (2007) *Culture, Identity, and Islamic Schooling. A Philosophical Approach*, New York: Palgrave Macmillan.

Merry, M. S. (2013) *Equality, Citizenship, and Segregation. A Defence of Segregation*, Houndsmills: Palgrave Macmillan.

Milligan, J. A. (2008) 'Islam and Education Policy Reform in the Southern Philippines', *Asia Pacific Journal of Education*, 28, 4, 369–81.

Millington, B., Vertinsky, P., Ellexis, B. and Wilson, B. (2008) 'Making Chinese-Canadian Masculinities in Vancouver's Physical Education Curriculum', *Sport, Education and Society*, 13, 2, 195–214.

Mills, C. W. (2007) 'Multiculturalism as / and / or Anti-racism', in Laden, A. S. and Owen, D. (eds) *Multiculturalism and Political Theory*, Cambridge: Cambridge University Press, 89–114.

Mirza, H. S. (2009) *Race, Gender and Educational Desire. Why Black Women Succeed and Fail*, London: Routledge.

Modood, T. (2005) *Multicultural Politics. Racism, Ethnicity and Muslims in Britain*, Edinburgh: Edinburgh University Press.

Modood. T. (2007) *Multiculturalism*, Cambridge: Polity Press.

Modood, T. (2008) 'Remaking Multiculturalism, Post 7/7', in Eade, J., Barrett, M., Flood, C. and Race, R. (eds) *Advancing Multiculturalism, Post 7/7*, Newcastle-Upon-Tyne: Cambridge Scholars Publishing, 135–48.

Modood, T. (2011) 'Multiculturalism and Integration: Struggling with Confusions', in Mahamdallie, H. (Ed.) *Defending Multiculturalism*, London: Bookmarks Publications, 61–76.

Modood, T. (2012) *Post-Immigration 'Difference' and Integration*, London: The British Academy.

Modood, T. (2nd ed.) (2013) *Multiculturalism*, Cambridge: Polity Press.

Modood, T., Berthous, R., Lakey, J., Nazroo, J., Smith, P., Virdee, S. and Beishon, S. (1997) *Ethnic Minorities in Britain. Diversity and Disadvantage*, London: Policy Studies Institute.

Moore, R. (2004) 'Cultural Capital: Objective Probability and the Cultural Arbitrary', *British Journal of Sociology of Education*, 25, 4, 445–56.

Morris, N. (2003) *The Politics of English Elementary School Finance, 1833–1870*, Lewiston: Edwin Mellon Press.

Mullard, C. (1983) 'The Racial Code: Its Features, Rules and Change', in Barton, L. and Walker, S. (eds) *Race, Class and Education*, Beckenham: Croom Helm, 139–65.

Mulvaney, M. (1984) 'Introduction – Multicultural Education in the Primary School', in Straker-Welds, M. (ed.) *Education for a Multicultural Society. Case Studies in ILEA Schools*, London: Bell & Hyman, 25–33.

Murphy, P. and Hall, K. (2008) *Learning and Practice. Agency and Identities*. London: Open University and Sage.

Neal, M. A. (2006) *New Black Man*, New York: Routledge.

Nicholl, B. and McClellan, R. (2008) '"We're All in This Game Whether We Like It or Not to Get a Number of As to Cs": Design and Technology Teachers' Struggles to Implement Creativity and Performativity Policies', *British Educational Research Journal*, 34, 5, 585–600.

Nieto, S. (2010) *The Light in Their Eyes. Creating Multicultural Learning Communities*, New York: Teachers College Press.

Nieto, S. and Bode, P. (5th ed.) (2008) *Affirming Diversity. The Sociopolitical Context of Multicultural Education*, Boston: Pearson and Allyn and Bacon.

Nombuso, D. S. and Dragana, M. (2007) 'In Pursuit of Being Canadian: Examining the Challenges of Culturally Relevant Education in Teacher Education Programs', *Race, Ethnicity and Education*, 10, 2, 155–75.

Norton-Taylor, R. (ed.) (1999) *The Colour of Justice. Based on the Transcripts of The Stephen Lawrence Inquiry*, London: Oberon Books.

Ochea-Becker, A. S. (2nd ed.) (2007) *Democratic Education for Social Studies. An Issues-Centered Decision Making Curriculum*, Greenwich: Information Age Publishing.

Office for Standards in Education (OFSTED) (2013) 'Citizenship Consolidated? A Survey of Citizenship in Schools between 2009 and 2012'. Available at http://www.ofsted.gov.uk/resources/citzenship-con-solidated-survey-of-citizenship-schools-between-2009-and-2012, last accessed 28th October 2013.

Office of Qualifications and Examinations Regulation (OfQual) (2014) 'About Us' http://ofqual.gov.uk/about-us/, last accessed 10th April 2014.

Okin, S. M. (2005) 'Multiculturalism and Feminism: No Simple Question, No Simple Answers', in Eisenberg, A. and Spiner-Halev, J. (eds) *Minorities within Minorities. Equality, Rights and Diversity*, Cambridge: Cambridge University Press, 67–89.

Olssen, M. (2004) 'From the Crick Report to the Parekh Report: Multiculturalism: Cultural Difference and Democracy – the Re-visioning of Citizenship Education', *British Journal of Sociology of Education*, 25, 2, 179–92.

Open Society Institute (2005) *Muslims in the UK. Policies for Engaged Citizens*, Budapest: European Union Monitoring and Advocacy Prográm.

Osler, A. (2008) 'Citizenship Education and the Ajegbo Report: Re-imaging a Cosmopolitan Nation', *London Review of Education*, 6, 1, 11–25.

Osler, A. (2009) 'Patriotism, Multiculturalism and Belonging: Political Discourse and the Teaching of History', *Educational Review*, 61, 1, 85–100.

Osler, A. and Starkey, H. (2005) *Changing Citizenship. Democracy and Inclusion in Education*, Maidenhead: Open University Press.

Pang, V. O., Nembhard, J. G. and Holowach, K. (2006) 'What is Multicultural Education? Principles and New Directions', in Pang, V. O. (ed.) *Principles and Practices of Multicultural Education*, Westport: Praeger Perspectives, 23–44.

Parekh, B. (1986) 'The Concept of Multi-Cultural Education', in Modgil, S., Verma, G. K., Mallick, K. and Modgil, C. (eds) *Multicultural Education. The Interminable Debate*, Lewes: Falmer Press, 19–32.

Parekh, B. (1988a) 'The Swann Report and Ethnic Minority Achievement', in Verma, G. and Pumfrey, P. (eds) *Educational Attainments. Issues and Outcomes in Multicultural Education*, Lewes: Falmer Press, 64–73.

Parekh, B. (1988b) 'Some Thoughts on Multicultural Education', in Taylor B. (ed.) *'Better To Light A Candle . . . ' More Multicultural Education* (Perspectives 39), School of Education, University of Exeter, 10–18.

Parekh, B. (2000) *Rethinking Multiculturalism. Cultural Diversity and Political Theory*, Harvard: Harvard University Press.

Parekh, B. (2008) *A New Politics of Identity, Political Principles for an Interdependent World*, Houndsmills: Palgrave Macmillan.

Parekh, B. (2011) *Talking Politics. Bhikhu Parekh in Conversation with Ramin Jahanbegloo*, Oxford: Oxford University Press.

Parker-Jenkins, M., Hartas, D. and Irving, B. A. (2005) *In Good Faith. Schools, Religion and Public Funding*, Aldershot: Ashgate.

Parsons, C. (2008) Race Relations Legislation, Ethnicity and Disproportionality in Social Exclusions in England, *Cambridge Journal of Education*, 38, 3, 401–19.

Pathak, P. (2007) 'The Trouble with David Goodhart's Britain', *Political Quarterly*, 78, 2, 261–71.

Pathak, P. (2008) *The Future of Multicultural Britain*, Edinburgh: Edinburgh University Press.

Pattie, C., Seyd, P. and Whitely, P. (2004) *Citizenship in Britain. Values, Participation and Democracy*, Cambridge: Cambridge University Press.

Personal Social Health and Economic Education (PSHE) (2010) PSHE Education – Working Definitions, www.pshe-association.org.uk.content.aspx?CategoryID=1043, last accessed 1st June 2010.

Phillips, A. (2007) *Multiculturalism without Culture*, Princeton: Princeton University Press.

Phillips, D. and Schweisfurth, M. (2007) *Comparative and International Education: An Introduction to Theory, Method, and Practice*, London: Continuum.

Phillips, T. (2005) 'After 7/7: Sleepwalking to Segregation', Speech given by CRE Chair Trevor Phillips at the Manchester Council for Community Relations, www.cre.gov.uk/default.aspx?textonly= 0&LocID=0hgnew07s@RefLocID=ohg00900c002@Lang+EN&htm, last accessed 27th August 2009.

Pilkington, A. (2003) *Racial Disadvantage and Ethnic Diversity in Britain*, Houndsmills: Palgrave Macmillan.

Piller, I. (2010) 'What Did Angela Merkel Really Say?' http://www.languageonthemove.com/language-globalization/what-did-angela-merkel-really-say, last accessed 14th March 2014.

Pollard, A., Anderson, J., Maddock, M., Swaffield, S., Warin, J. and Warwick, P. (3rd ed.) (2008) *Reflective Teaching*, London: Continuum.

Pollock, M. (2004) *Colormute. Race Talk Dilemmas in an American School*, Princeton: Princeton University Press.

Pollock, M. (2008) *Because of Race. How Americans Debates Harm and Opportunity in Our Schools*, Princeton: Princeton University Press.

Pratt-Adams, A., Maguire, M. and Burn, E. (2010) *Changing Urban Education*, London: Continuum.

Preston, J. (2009) 'Preparing for Emergencies: Citizenship Education, "Whiteness" and Pedagogies of Security', *Citizenship Studies*, 13, 2, 187–200.

Pring, R. (2005) 'Faith Schools: Can They Be Justified?' in Gardner, R., Cairns, J. and Lawton, D. (eds) *Faith Schools. Consensus or Conflict?* Abingdon: RoutledgeFalmer, 51–60.

QCDA (2009b) *National Curriculum – Citizenship Key Stage 4, Statutory Content*, http://curriculum.qcda.gov.uk/key-stages-3-and-4/subjects/citizenship/keystage4/index.aspx, last accessed 25th August 2009.

QCDA (2009c) *Promoting Racial Equality*, www.qcda.gov.uk/22479.aspx, last accessed 29th August 2009.

Qualifications and Curriculum Authority (QCA) (1998) *Education for Citizenship and the Teaching of Democracy in School*, London: Department for Education and Employment.

Qualifications and Curriculum Development Agency (QCDA) (2009a) *National Curriculum – Citizenship Key Stage 2, Non-Statutory Content*, http://curriculum.qcda.gov.uk/key-stages-1-and-2/ subjects/citizenship /keystage2/index.aspx?return=/search/index.aspx%3FfldSiteSearch%3DCitizenship+-+Key+stage+2, last accessed 25th August 2009.

Race, R. (2001a) 'Analysing Ethnic Education Policy Making in England and Wales', *Sheffield Online Papers in Social Research*, Number 5, www.shef.ac.uk/uni/academic/r-z/socst/shop/race_article.pdf, last accessed 10th July 2009.

Race, R. (2001b) 'Bureaucratic Rationality, Flux or Neutrality? Analysing the Relationship between Civil Servants and Politicians Affecting Education Policy, 1970–1974'. PhD Thesis, Keele University, United Kingdom.

Race, R. (2006) 'Using Educational Research When Conceptually Developing the *Good Society*', *British Education Research Journal*, 32, 1, 131–43.

Race, R. (2007) 'Between Past Failure and Future Promise. Racial Discrimination and the Education System, UN Chronicle, XLIV, 3, 28–30, www.un.org/Pubs/chronical/2007/ issue3/0307p28.html#, last accessed 10th July 2009.

Race, R. (2008a) 'Introduction', in Eade, J., Barrett, M., Flood, C. and Race, R. (eds) *Advancing Multiculturalism, Post 7/7*, Newcastle-Upon-Tyne: Cambridge Scholars Publishing, 1–6.

Race, R. (2008b) 'Advancing Multiculturalism, Post 7/7', Paper presented to the American Education Research Association Conference. New York City, 24th March 2008.

Race, R. (2008c) 'Teaching Diversity to Prevent Terrorism?' Paper presented to the conference, '*Terrorism, Human Rights and Media: Finding the Balance*', Brunel University, 7th July 2008.

Race, R. (2009a) 'Troyna Revisited: Conceptually Examining Anti-racism and Multiculturalism within Education' in Pilkington, A. Housee, S. and Hylton, K. (eds) *Race(ing) Forward: Transitions in Theorising 'Race' in Education*, Birmingham: Higher Education Academy, C-SAP Monograph Number 11, 167–83.

Race, R. (2009b) 'The Politics of Integration Multiculturalism and Citizenship Education Policy', Paper presented to the CRONEM 2009 / AHRC Conference, Surrey University, 11th June 2009.

Race, R. (2009c) 'If Multiculturalism Still Matters in Education, What Is Its Future?' Paper presented to the British Education Research Association Conference, Manchester University, 4th September 2009.

Race, R. (2011) 'Integrationist to Citizenship Education Policy within England: A Forward Movement or a Backward Step', in Barrett, M., Flood, C. and Eade, J. (eds) *Nationalism, Ethnicity, Citizenship. Multidisciplinary Perspectives*, Newcastle-Upon-Tyne: Cambridge Scholars Publishing, 181–94.

Race, R. (2012) 'The Warning of the Integrationist Alternative for Education and the Multicultural Backlash', in Wright, H. K., Singh, M. and Race, R. (eds) *Precarious International Multicultural Education*, Rotterdam: Sense Publishers, 333–46.

Race, R. (2014) 'The Multicultural Dilemma, the Integrationist Consensus and the Consequences for Advancing Race and Ethnicity within Education', in Race, R. and Lander, V. (eds) *Advancing Race and Ethnicity in Education*, Houndsmills: Palgrave Macmillan, 210–29.

Race, R. and Lander, V. (eds) (2014) *Advancing Race and Ethnicity in Education*, Houndsmills: Palgrave Macmillan.

Ramadan, T. (2009) *Radical Reform: Islamic Ethics and Liberation*, Oxford: Oxford University Press.

Ramsey, P. R. (3rd ed.) (2004) *Teaching and Learning in a Diverse World*, New York: Teachers College Press.

Ratcliffe, P. (2012) '"Community Cohesion": Reflections on a Flawed Paradigm', *Critical Social Policy*, 32, 2, 262–81.

Ravitch, S. M., Roeser, R. and Girard, B. J. (2005) 'Critical Multicultural Teacher Reflections. Counter- narratives to Images of the White Male Blockhead', in Peters-Davies, N. and Shultz, J. (eds) *Challenges of Multicultural Education. Teaching and Taking Diversity Courses*, Boulder, CO: Paradigm Publishers, 121–47.

Reed, L. R. (1995) 'Reconceptualising Equal Opportunities in the 1990s: A Study of Radical Teacher Culture in Transition', in Griffiths, M. and Troyna, B. (eds) *Antiracism, Culture and Social Justice in Education*, Stoke-on-Trent: Trentham Books, 77–96.

Reich, R. (2002) *Bridging Liberalism and Multiculturalism in American Education*, Chicago: Chicago University Press.

Rex, J. (1997) 'Multiculturalism and Antiracism Reconsidered', in Sikes, P. and Rizvi, F. (eds) (1997) *Researching Race and Social Justice in Education. Essays in Honour of Barry Troyna*, Stoke-on-Trent: Trentham Books, 109–18.

Rex, J. (2008) 'Ethnic-Identity in a Multicultural Society', in Eade, J., Barrett, M., Flood, C. and Race, R. (eds) *Advancing Multiculturalism, Post 7/7*, Newcastle-Upon-Tyne: Cambridge Scholars Publishing, 29–41.

Richards, C. (forthcoming) *Young People, Popular Culture and Education*, London: Continuum.

Richardson, B. (ed.) (2005) *Tell It Like It Is: How Our Schools Fail Black Children,* Stoke-on-Trent: Trentham Books.

Ritzer, G. (2010) *Globalization: A Basic Text*, Oxford: Wiley-Blackwell.

Rmaji, G. (2009) *Researching Race: Theory, Method and Analysis*, Maidenhead: Open University Press.

Robinson, A. M. (2007) *Multiculturalism and the Foundations of Meaningful Life. Reconciling Autonomy, Identity and Community,* Vancouver: University of British Columbia Press.

Roisin, C. (2007) 'Student Teachers' Perception of Their Role and Responsibilities as Catholic Educators', *European Journal of Teacher Education*, 30, 4, 445–65.

158 Bibliography

Runnymede Trust (2000) *The Future of Multi-Ethnic Britain*, Report of the Commission on the Future of Multi-ethnic Britain, Chair Bhikhu Parekh, The Parekh Report, London, Profile Books.

Ryan, J. (1999) *Race and Ethnicity in Multi-Ethnic Schools*, Clevedon: Multilingual Matters.

Sagger, S. and Somerville, W. (2012) 'Building a British Model of Integration in an Era of Immigration', http://www.migrationpolicy.org/research/building-british-model-integration-era-immigration-policy-lessons-government, last accessed 30th April 2014.

Saili, F. and Hoosain, R. (2001) 'Multicultural Education: History, Issues and Practices', in Salili, F. and Hoosain, R. (eds) *Multicultural Education: Issues, Policies and Practices*, Greenwich: Information Age, 1–14.

Santoro, N. (2007) '"Outsiders" and "Others": "Different" Teachers Teaching in Culturally Diverse Classrooms', *Teachers and Teaching: Theory and Practice*, 31, 1, 81–97.

Santoro, N. (2009) 'Teaching in Culturally Diverse Contexts: What Knowledge about "Self" and "Others" Do Teachers Need?', *Journal of Education for Teaching: International Research and Pedagogy*, 35, 1, 33–45.

Saunders, D. (2009) 'France on the Knife-edge of Religion: Commemorating the Centenary of the Law of 9 December 1905 on the Separation of Church and State', in Brahm Levey, G. and Modood, T. (eds) *Secularism, Religion and Multicultural Citizenship*, Cambridge: Cambridge University Press, 56–81.

Scarman, Lord. (1982) *The Scarman Report. The Brixton Disorders, 10–12 April 1981, Presented to Parliament by the Secretary of Sate for the Home Department by Command of Her Majesty November 1981*, London: Penguin Books.

Sen, A. (2006) *Identity and Violence. The Illusion of Destiny*, London: Allen Lane.

Sewell, T. (2000) *Black Masculinities and Schooling. How Black Boys Survive Modern Schooling*, Stoke-on-Trent: Trentham Books.

Shaules, J. (2007) *Deep Culture. The Hidden Challenges of Global Living*, Clevedon: Multilingual Matters.

Singh, B. R. (1992) 'Teaching Methods that Enhance Human Dignity, Self-Respect and Academic Achievement', in Lynch, J., Modgil, C. and Modgil, S. (eds) *Cultural Diversity and the Schools. Volume 2: Prejudice, Polemic or Progress?* London: Falmer Press, 207–30.

Singh, G. (1993) *Equality and Education*, Derby: Albrighton Publications.

Sleeter, C. E. and Grant, C. A. (5th ed.) (2006) *Making Choices for Multicultural Education. Five Approaches to Race, Class, and Gender*, New York: John Wiley and Sons Limited.

Smith, D. and Greenfields, M. (2012) 'Housed Gypsies and Travellers in the UK: Work, Exclusion and Adaptation', *Race and Class*, 53, 3, 48–64.

Smith, J. (2009) '"The Enemy Within?": The Clergyman and the English School Boards, 1870–1902', *History of Education*, 38, 1, 133–49.

Somers, M. R. (2008) *Genealogies of Citizenship. Markets, Statelessness, and the Right to Have Rights*, Cambridge: Cambridge University Press.

Song, S. (2007) *Justice, Gender, and the Politics of Multiculturalism*, Cambridge: Cambridge University Press.

Steinburg, S. R. (ed.) (2009) *Diversity and Multiculturalism: A Reader*, New York: Peter Lang.

Steinberg, S. R. and Kincheloe, J. L. (2001) 'Setting the Context for Critical Multi /Interculturalism. The Power Blocs of Class Elitism, White Supremacy, and Patriarchy', in Steinberg, S. R. (ed.) *Multi / Intercultural Conversations: A Reader*, New York: Peter Lang, 3–30.

Stepan, A. and Taylor, C. (eds) (2014) *Boundaries of Toleration*, New York: Columbia University Press.

Stephens, W. B. (1998) *Education in Britain, 1750–1914*, Houndsmills: Macmillan.

Stevenson, J. (2014) 'Internationalisation and Religious Inclusion in United Kingdom Higher Education', *Higher Education Quarterly*, How do you behave after the viva? 68, 1, 44–64.

Stringer, M., Irwing, P., Giles, M., McClenahan, C., Wilson, R. and Hunter, J. A. (2009) 'Intergroup Contact, Friendship Quality and Political Attitudes in Integrated and Segregated Schools in Northern Ireland', *British Journal of Educational Psychology*, 79, 2, 239–57.

Tang, S. Y. F. and Choi, P. L. (2009) 'Teachers' Professional Lives and Continuing Professional Development in Changing Times', *Educational Review*, 61, 1, 1–18.

Tatum, B. D. (2007) *Can We Talk about Race? And Other Conversations in an Era of School Resegregation*, Boston: Beacon Press.

Taylor, M. J. (1987) *Chinese Pupils in Britain. A Review of Research into the Education of Pupils of Chinese Origin*, Windsor: NFER-Nelson.

Taylor, M. J. (1988) *World's Apart? A Review of Research into the Education of Pupils of Cypriot, Italian, Ukrainian and Vietnamese Origin, Liverpool Blacks and Gypsies*, Windsor: NFER-Nelson.

Thomas, E. (2005) 'Globalisation, Cultural Diversity and Teacher Education', in Cullingford, C. and Gunn, S. (eds) *Globalisation, Education and Culture Shock*, Aldershot: Ashgate, 138–56.

Todd, R. (1991) *Education in a Multicultural Society*, London: Cassell.

Tomlinson, S. (1983) *Ethnic Minorities in British Schools. A Review of the Literature, 1960–1982*, London: Heinemann Educational Books.

Tomlinson, S. (1986) 'Ethnicity and Educational Achievement', in Modgil, S., Verma, G. K., Mallick, K. and Modgil, C. (eds) *Multicultural Education. The Interminable Debate*, Lewes: Falmer Press, 181–94.

Tomlinson, S. (1990) *Multicultural Education in White Schools*, London: B. T. Batsford Limited.

Tomlinson, S. (2004) 'The Education of Migrants and Minorities in Britain', in Luchtenburg, S. (ed.) *Migration, Education and Change*, London: New York, 86–102.

Tomlinson, S. (2008) *Race and Education. Policy and Politics in Britain*, Maidenhead: McGraw Hill.

Touraine, A. (2000) *Can We Live Together?* Cambridge: Polity Press.

Tournon, J. (2013) 'The Importance of Citizenship Criteria: Andre Suares and Jewishness in Germany between Ethnicity, Religion and Nationalism', in Williams, M. H. (ed.) *The Multicultural Dilemma. Migration, Ethnic Politics, and State Intermediation*, Abingdon: Routledge, 100–18.

Triandafyllidou, A., Modood, T. and Zapata-Barrero, R. (2006) 'European Challenges to Multicultural Citizenship: Muslims, Secularism and Beyond', in Modood, T., Triandafyllidou, A. and Zapata-Barrero, R. (eds) *Multiculturalism, Muslims and Citizenship. A European Approach*, London: Routledge, 1–22.

Troman, G., Jeffrey, B. and Raggi, A. (2007) 'Creativity and Performativity Policies in Primary School Cultures', *Journal of Education Policy*, 22, 5, 549–72.

Troyna, B. (1987a) 'A Conceptual Overview of Strategies to Combat Racial Inequality in Education: Introductory Essay', in Tronya, B. (ed.) *Racial Inequality in Education*, London: Tavistock Publishers, 1–10.

Troyna, B. (1987b) '"Swann's Song": The Origins, Ideology and Implications of *Education for All*', in Chivers, T. S. (ed.) *Race and Culture in Education. Issues Arising from the Swann Committee Report*, Windsor: NFER-Nelson, 26–43.

Troyna, B. (1991) 'Underachievers or Underrated? The Experience of Pupils of South Asian Origin in a Secondary School', *British Educational Research Journal*, 17, 4, 361–76.

Troyna, B. (1992) 'Can You See the Join? An Historical Analysis on Multicultural and Antiracist Education Policies', in Gill, D., Mayor, B. and Blair, M. (eds) *Racism and Education. Structures and Strategies*, London: Open University with Sage, 63–91,

Troyna, B. (1993) *Racism and Education*, Buckingham: Open University Press.

Troyna, B. (1995) 'The Local Management of Schools and Racial Equality', in Tomlinson, S. and Craft, M. (eds) *Ethnic Relations and Schooling. Policy and Practice in the 1990s*, London: Athlone, 140–54.

Troyna, B. (1998) '"The Whites of My Eyes, Nose, Ears . . . ": A Reflexive Account of "Whiteness" in Race-related Research', in Connolly, P. and Troyna, B. (eds) *Researching Racism in Education. Politics, Theory and Practice*, Buckingham: Open University Press, 95–108.

Troyna, B. and Williams, J. (1986) *Racism, Education and the State: The Racialisation of Education Policy*, Beckenham: Croom Helm.

Tulloch, J. (2006) *One Day in July: Experiencing 7/7*, London: Little, Brown Group Book.

Tyack, D. (2003) *Seeking Common Ground. Public Schools in a Diverse Society*, Harvard: Harvard University Press.

Urrieta, L. (2006) 'Community Identity Discourse and the Heritage Academy: Color-blind Educational Policy and White Supremacy', *International Journal of Qualitative Studies in Education*, 19, 4, 455–76.

van Houtte, M. and Stevens, P. A. J. (2009) '"School Ethnic Composition and Students" Integration Outside and Inside Schools in Belgium', *Sociology of Education*, 82, 3, 217–39.

Verma, G. K. (2007) 'Diversity and Multicultural Education: Cross-cutting Issues and Concepts', in Verma, G. K., Bagley, C. R. and Mohan Jha, M. (eds) *International Perspectives on Educational Diversity and Inclusion. Studies from America, Europe and India*, London: Routledge, 21–30.

Walford, G. (2008) 'Faith-based Schools in England after Ten Years of Tony Blair', *Oxford Review of Education*, 34, 6, 689–99.

Wasmer, M. (2013) 'Public Debates and Public Opinion on Multiculturalism in Germany', in Taras, R. (ed.) *Challenging Multiculturalism. European Models of Diversity*, Edinburgh: Edinburgh University Press, 163–89.

Watkins, C. and Mortimore, P. (1999) 'Pedagogy: What Do We Know?', in Mortimore, P. (ed.) *Understanding Pedagogy and Its Impact on Learning*, London: Paul Chapman Publishing, 1–20.

Watson, C. W. (2000) *Multiculturalism*, Buckingham: Open University Press.

Weil, D. K. (1998) *Towards a Critical Multicultural Literacy. Theory and Practice for Education for Liberation*, New York: Peter Lang.

Wells, K. (2009) *Childhood in a Global Perspective*, Cambridge: Polity Press.

White, J. (ed.) (2004) *Rethinking the School Curriculum, Values, Aims and Purposes*, London: RoutledgeFalmer.

Williams, M. H. (2013) *The Multicultural Dilemma: Migration, Ethnic Politics, and State Intermediation*, Abingdon: Routledge.

Woodman, D. (2009) 'Questioning Citizenship', Roehampton: Roehampton University, www. roe-hampton.ac.uk/crucible/programmes/index.html, last accessed 25th August 2009.

Yeshanew, T., Schagen, I. and Evans, S. (2008) 'Faith Schools and Pupils' Progress through Primary Education', *Educational Studies*, 34, 5, 511–26.

Young, M. (1958) *The Rise of the Meritocracy 1870–2033: An Essay on Education and Equality*, London: Thames and Hudson.

Yuval-Davis, N. (1992) 'Fundamentalism, and Women in Britain', in Donald, J. and Rattansi, A. (eds) *'Race', Culture & Difference*, London: Open University Press with Sage, 278–92.

Zapata-Barrero, R. and Gropas, R. (2012) 'Active Immigrants in Multicultural Contexts: Democratic Challenges in Europe', in Trinandafyyidou, A., Modood, T. and Meer, N. (eds) *European Multiculturalisms. Cultural, Religious and Ethnic Challenges*, Edinburgh: Edinburgh University Press, 167–91.

Author Index

Subject Index

Page numbers in **bold** denote tables.